PRAISE FOR

Prone To Wander

"*Prone to Wander* guides readers across six continents with wit, faith, and wonder. The author interweaves her personal discovery of patience, an embrace of myriad cultures, and the power of community into a tapestry of global experience. Laventure's 'unexpected core of boldness and thirst for adventure' propels her into Tolkienian adventures as she stretches boundaries and confronts fears in faraway lands. From a pilgrimage to Bono's Ireland home to sipping mojitos in Havana to exploring the Shire in New Zealand, you'll end up asking yourself how you can be more courageous. *Prone to Wander* stands as a powerful testament to the transformative nature of exploration. It reminds us that our greatest discoveries about the world and ourselves lie beyond the familiar."

—Cindy Cunningham, author of *Wild Woman:*
A Memoir in Pieces

"LaVenture is an ideal traveling companion! Her gallivanting tales from around the globe are as fun to read as they are inspiring. From hunting for Bono in Dublin to dining on crocodile in Africa, LaVenture's international adventures will have you hunting for your passport, signing up for classes at community college or both!"

—Anne Soffee, author *of Snake Hips: Belly Dancing* and
How I Found True Love

"Written by a true legend, this memoir describes the development and implementation of one of the most well-known community college international education programs in the nation, which exists in rural North Carolina of all places. It elegantly intertwines narrative about religion, body image, commonality and difference, life and death, and living life with meaning and purpose, all while describing a dazzling array of locations around the world. Readers with previous international experiences will immediately resonate with the book's descriptions of encountering a dramatically different culture only to find yourself at home, fearlessly striking out into the unknown only to find familiarity, and finding God not only in houses of worship across faith traditions around the world, but also U2 concerts and hostel reception areas. This book is a must-read for international educators and community college leaders."

—Melissa Whatley, PhD, Assistant Professor of
Higher Education, William & Mary

Prone to Wander

A Memoir

Suzanne LaVenture

Sibylline
DIGITAL FIRST

**Sibylline
Press**

For Craig, my constant compass and favorite husband

CLOISTER DRIVE – THE PAST IS PROLOGUE

I was born into a small world, one whose borders could never stretch to fill the universe inside me. A crack first appeared in the protective dome of my life the night Tori and Tina's daddy died. My sister Cindy and I were sleepy-eyed and confused in our twin beds when Tori and Tina appeared in our bedroom in the middle of the night. Something bad had happened. Mom deposited our friends with us and then hurried back next door to comfort Mrs. Scott and wait for the ambulance with our dad. We two pairs of sisters were interwoven in age: I was eleven, Tori was ten, Cindy nine, and Tina eight. We thought our world was safe.

Mr. Scott was the scariest thing we knew. Cindy and I saw him yelling red-faced at Tori and Tina and we knew about the spankings. He was nothing like our goofy father, master of silly puns and dad jokes. We roller-skated in the Scotts' basement on occasion, but never played upstairs. Mrs. Scott's piercing blue eyes did not radiate kindness either, her pinched face and bee-hive hairdo were as tight as her housekeeping. The pair worked at the Food World down the street, blasted country music, and attended a Baptist church even more conservative than our own. One morning, for reasons lost to time, Mr. Scott drove me to school in his red Ford Pinto. He sang along to *Jolene*, dog tags swaying around his neck, as he glanced at me shifting uncomfortably in the rearview mirror as I worried that he might talk to me.

Shortly after her husband's death, a grocery store manager appeared in Mrs. Scott's life. Cindy and I immediately concluded she had killed Mr. Scott because of his meanness. Our theory was possibly linked to the debut of the *Helter Skelter* mini-series. We weren't allowed to watch it, but our school friends relayed every gory detail of the Manson murders. When we shared our theory with our mother, she shook her head, telling us how distraught Mrs. Scott had been. The shock and horror were real. Mrs. Scott fainted when the ambulance driver told her that her husband was gone. Mom provided the conclusive detail that Tori and Tina's dresses were hanging on their bedroom door frame, pressed and ready for Sunday School the following morning. Mrs. Scott was not expecting her thirty-four-year-old husband to die in his sleep. There was no autopsy; everyone (except for Cindy and me) assumed the death was due to a brain aneurysm.

In the days that followed, the four of us girls sat under the ground-sweeping branches of the cedar tree that separated our driveways. This secret pine cathedral sheltered us from the outside world. In those days, kids played outside, generous trees and forts of rotting wood providing shade and rest. Cindy was the Queen of the Neighborhood, running the street like a petite mob boss with a pixie haircut, while I continuously attempted to slink inside the house to read stories about faraway lands. We didn't know what to say to Tori and Tina, but we sat with them, sunlight filtering through the lacy branches. We gathered a pile honeysuckle flowers from a nearby vine and placed them in our circle. We snipped off the green tips of the white and pale orange flowers, pulling the tube-like petal through the flower to deposit a drop of nectar on our tongues. We didn't know what to say, but we knew what to do.

I knew dreadful things happened in novels, but books were make-believe. My world consisted of my street, my classroom, and my church. If bad stuff could happen on Cloister Drive, I wasn't safe anywhere. My mother tried her best to cloister Cindy and me; to keep us from the sinful world. Our TV watching was strictly monitored. We weren't allowed to watch the first season of *Happy Days* because of the Fonz's amorous proclivities. Shows like *Maude, All in the Family,* and *M*A*S*H* were strictly off limits. We always wore slips under our dresses so no one could see the outline of our child legs in the sunlight. I burned with embarrassment when a song like Rod Stewart's *Do Ya Think I'm Sexy?* came on the radio.

Devout Southern Baptists, we attended Sunday School and Worship every week and returned on Sunday evening for Training Union. I gustily sang hymns about fountains of blood washing away guilty stains. Mysterious phrases like *alpha and omega, ancient of days,* and *bright morning star* evoked deep echoes of recognition inside me. A champion at Sunday night Bible drills, I was always able to find the chapter and verse before any adult, stepping forth to read while others were still flipping pages. *Attention*! (Feet together, shoulders back, hands at sides). *Draw swords*! (Bring Bible to waist, one hand flat on the bottom, one hand flat on the cover.) *Charge*! (Find assigned chapter and verse as fast as you can). Once your finger locates the verse, step forward and begin reading. Adding a competitive component to the spiritual life suited me well since I excelled at the task. I was the Queen of Bible drills.

Wednesday nights were reserved for the house of God as well. Supper was served—sandwiches or a potluck or a prepared meal—and then it was off to Girls in Action, a missions-focused discipleship group for girls in grades one through six. We learned about brave missionaries like Lottie Moon who boldly answered God's call to serve the people of China. I spent a lot of my free time at home earning GA badges, scanning the activity book for easy to complete tasks to cross off my list with a freshly sharpened pencil. Mom wasn't great at ironing the badges onto my vest, but I didn't mind. Accomplishment was its own reward, achievements compensated for my deficit in social class and my excess in body weight. I was determined to prove that I was just as good as anyone else.

The highlight of my summer was Vacation Bible School. We'd spend a week playing and crafting and studying faraway lands like Botswana. We glued macaroni to construction paper and knotted macramé wall hangings, though I don't remember what the crafts had to do with Botswana. I was intrigued by the idea of such a different country existing in the real world, a place where cheetahs and crocodiles and elephants gallivanted about with no bars to restrain them. Without a doubt, my desire to visit Africa had its seeds in the church basement.

Our school life was sheltered, too. In second grade, my evil but astute teacher Mrs. Adams recommended that I be tested for the gifted program, which was limited to fifty students per grade across the entire county. The School Board plucked rising third-graders from different schools like tasty morsels out of a mediocre dish and dropped us into a single school, split into two classes of AT students per grade. A year later, Cindy joined me in this new world of the intellectual elite, skipping a grade to boot. We were the only kids from the Southside. Most of our classmates were white and wealthy; Cindy and I were Dickensian waifs in comparison.

My heart filled with longing for the baby blue Levi corduroys, striped rugby shirts, and Wallabies the other kids wore daily. I hated my pretty plus jeans from Sears. And yet, nerds (a label I now proudly claim) are generally nice and well-mannered people. I had plenty of friends and no one looked down on me, though it didn't quell my burning need to prove I was just as good as they were. Voracious readers all of us, we loved to listen to our teacher reading us books about Mars and Middle-earth and the Russian Tsars. More seeds planted in my prone-to-wander heart.

In every way, I was raised to be protected from the world. The World was something to be feared, dangerous to your moral, spiritual, and physical well-being. But like Eve, I was curious. I had a hunger for knowledge. I wanted to know *everything*. Mr. Scott's death showed me that I wasn't safe in the cocoon, that the world could find me no matter how hidden I was from it. I started to worry that my own parents could die, or that the woods behind our house could catch on fire, or that nuclear war could destroy us all. If being sheltered couldn't protect me, what was the point of hiding? Under all the layers of good girl chubbiness and nerdiness, I possessed a surprising core of boldness and thirst for adventure. My big brain and religious instruction made me confident of always being right and the necessary corollary of always doing right. God was on my side. In addition to all the dangers in the world my mother warned me about, I suspected that there might be wonders as well.

It turns out that I was right.

COLOMBIA – ROMANCING THE STONE

Heartbreak ambushed me in my sophomore year of college. My high school sweetheart dumped me. The news arrived like the stab of a splintery stake to the heart. I couldn't breathe. Bile rose in my throat. An invisible knife twisted in my gut. I clutched my belly and rocked; the physical pain rivaled the emotional agony. I had loved him with everything I had.

I just needed to know why, believing I could fix things if I had the answer. He did not have an answer.

Several months after this first breakup, I was waiting on a rowdy group of revelers at the restaurant where I worked to pay my tuition. The Talking Heads blared in the smoke-filled restaurant and as I passed the partying table, a blond, green-eyed young man grabbed my arm, locked eyes with me, and proposed. I still struggled with my recent heartbreak, but I raised an eyebrow and said "Sure, why not?" I scribbled my number on a bev nap and finished my shift, dismissing the interaction as an intoxicated bit of nonsense. To my surprise, he called a few days later.

I threw up before our first date even though vomiting is something I avoid at all costs. I couldn't imagine being with another man. At the small, chic restaurant he had chosen for their renowned Mama's Chocolate Cake, I picked at a salad, partly because I was still on my depression diet and partly because the taste of vomit lingered in the back of my throat.

He invited me to go skiing for our second date and I accepted, excited for a travel adventure even though it was only a couple of hours away. Skiing was a disaster, but I must have looked cute. I went down the mountain mostly on my butt. We had sex that night and I cried. Peter was understanding; he knew I wasn't over my first boyfriend. I grieved for the loss of my first love. I grieved for the failed ideal of only having sex with the man I married. All my life the church had taught me that sex should only happen within marriage, but since I had already blown it, what did it matter?

A rebound relationship for both of us, we moved quickly into exclusivity. Peter struggled to let go of his former girlfriend and I obviously wasn't over my first love. We settled into a familiar intimacy and having a handsome new boyfriend helped me feel desirable and less like a reject. He taught me to drink red wine and Dom Perignon. He tried to teach me to ride horses – another disaster ending with the huge animal bucking me off its back. Peter worked at a lumber mill owned by his wealthy father and lived in an older apartment building with high ceilings and a screened porch. Despite our less-than-stellar first time, Peter and I had sexual chemistry. I would go to his apartment after finishing up at the restaurant, but I always left early in the morning to get ready for class at my place. One August day before the start of my junior year of college, I tiptoed from his apartment to my car as dawn broke over the historic West End. No one seemed to be awake for my walk of shame, but I kept an eye on the houses to my left and the open field to my right. You never knew what might happen.

The news shattered the morning's quiet. Death brushed by me again on its way to someone else nearby. Deborah Sykes, a young woman with a life full of promise, was found brutally murdered in the field next to my parked car. The horror of it was almost incomprehensible. Her violent death was a stark, terrifying reminder of the vulnerability women carry with us every day. It could have been any of us. It could have been me.

Fear, a silent and ever-present companion, shapes women's lives. We learn to navigate the world with a hypervigilance that men rarely experience. We carry our keys in our fists, we don't take walks after dark, we stash mace in our purses, and drape sweaters over our cleavage. Mainly, we fear what happens in the dark. Few of us fear danger on the morning commute on a sleepy, clear morning in a mid-size city in the South. Yet even the most guarded moments offer no true protection. A clear morning, a familiar path—safety in the world was still an illusion.

The Sykes case became a personal obsession to me. The injustice of her murder was compounded by the subsequent wrongful conviction of Daryl Hunt. His story, a testament to systemic failures and the enduring impact of violence, is a haunting echo of the original tragedy. Ten years after Sykes' murder, DNA proved Hunt was not the rapist, but he remained imprisoned for another decade before being found innocent. That morning in 1984 spawned one last tragedy: Hunt died of a self-inflicted gunshot a dozen years after his release from prison. Almost twenty years of prison for a murder he did not commit had taken its toll. He was another victim of the actual murderer, a man named Willard Brown.

These events forced me to confront the deep-rooted fears that shaped my life and the lives of countless women. It was also the beginning of a journey toward understanding and advocacy, a determination to create a world where people can live with less fear.

★ ★ ★

In late spring, Peter announced his decision to join the Coast Guard.

"What the hell?" I demanded.

I was not thrilled by the thought of my boyfriend living on a ship. I huffed to class, noticing a flier on a bulletin board: a scholarship competition to spend a semester at La Universidad de los Andes in Bogotá, Colombia. The deadline was that day. Whipping out some paper and a pen, I scribbled an essay, vindication coursing through my veins. *He'll leave? I'll leave!* When I learned I won the scholarship, I felt elated because I like winning. Then it dawned on me: *Oh shit, I have to spend a semester in Bogotá by myself.* But at least I wouldn't be sitting at home while Peter sailed off to who-knew-where.

When I informed my father that I had won a scholarship to Colombia, he asked me why I wanted to go to New York.

"Not Columbia," I informed him. "*Colombia*. South America."

"Oh," he replied. "Are you going to meet Juan Valdez?"

My father always found himself hilarious.

Months later, in a classroom high in the Andes, I laughed out loud when my Latin American History professor began to speak about Juan Valdez. Who knew Juan was a real person and not just the mustachioed, sombrero-wearing farmer leading a coffee-laden donkey around a grocery store in a television commercial? He really did pick his coffee bean by bean! Hence, the U.S. became Colombia's primary coffee market since Americans (including myself) prefer the smooth taste that results from only using ripe beans. Meanwhile, Europeans preferred Brazilian coffee since they harvest the ripe and unripe beans together, yielding a bitter flavor. This knowledge did not alleviate the sting of learning that free refills are a uniquely American concept. In Colombia, as in most countries, you must pay for each cup of coffee. At least it was cheap.

My host family lived on the outskirts of the city. The night I arrived, the husband picked me up from the airport and grunted as he carted my three giant, wheelless suitcases to his car. As a novice traveler, I had not yet learned the art of packing light. Upon arrival at their home, the wife served me a special dinner: a cow's tongue glistening with spots and veins. The meat wasn't sliced or disguised by gravy. A giant tongue ripped from a bovine's mouth sat on my plate and I was supposed to eat it. I struggled, not wanting to be rude but not wanting to throw up either. The only cow parts I consumed were hamburgers and a T-bone on incredibly special occasions. I cut up the tongue, feeling the knife slice through the tender flesh. Pushing my food around my plate, I declared *no tengo hambre*. I knew I should take a bite, but I just couldn't. I was embarrassed by my lack of manners. I wasn't culturally competent yet, but a good Southern girl knew that politeness is a cousin to kindness.

I offered to help with the dishes, but my hosts informed me that the maid would take care of that. Sweet, shy Fanny lived in a small room and kept the house immaculate. She ironed my jeans, pajamas, and towels, though I begged her not to. It took me a while to figure out I was supposed to wash my panties in the shower even though Fanny washed and ironed everything else. It felt weird to have someone serving me. Coming from a lower middle-class background, the idea of having help was as foreign to me as beef tongue for dinner. In Colombia, every middle-class family employed a *criada*. They were paid virtually nothing, so it wasn't a large expense, but I couldn't shake the discomfort of the class distinction. In the U.S. we at least pretend to believe that all people are created equal. I felt closer to Fanny than to the family, but she probably didn't feel the same about me.

For my hour's ride to the university, I had to take one of the jam-packed public buses for over a hundred blocks. I hailed a cab for the first week but realized that wasn't sustainable on my budget. Gathering my courage, I waited on the corner and flagged down the bus, people crammed into it like a giant clown car. By the end of my time in Bogotá, I would wedge one foot on the bottom step and ride hanging out the door until enough people got off that I could work my way onto the bus. This act of cultural assimilation taught me the vast human capacity for adaptation. The women in their high heels keeping their balance on the crazy bus rides never ceased to amaze me. That was a cultural norm I did not attempt to emulate.

I'm not sure why Colombian women wanted to attract attention from men because in my opinion they already got too much. On the bus, there was the disgusting practice known as *ponerle el rabo* where a man would shamelessly bounce his erection against you while you were trapped like a canned sardine. The allusion to Pin the Tail on the Donkey did not amuse me. On the streets, men you passed would toss out a *piropo* – a compliment or a catcall, depending on your perspective. Some of these comments were kindly tributes to one's beauty and others were significantly more vulgar. I found that a solid "Fuck you!" was a good response to either. I always enjoyed the confused expressions when the men realized I was an American; I loved being able to pass for Colombian.

Luckily, I made friends early on. During my first week at Uniandes, I was lurking around the Dean of International Students' office, trying to steal toilet paper since it was the only bathroom in Bogotá that had any. Outside, I noticed a red-haired student leaning against a post and smoking a cigarette. Perhaps I bummed a cigarette or asked him where he was from (Chicago), but no matter how that first day began, Seth and I soon hung out regularly along with a dark-haired, blue-eyed girl from Boston named Lisa. Our threesome helped me feel less lonely, but it also resulted in me speaking a lot more English than I should have. We hung out on campus and met up at bars and clubs on the weekends. Seth lived in an apartment with three Colombian dental students, one of whom had been an exchange student at his high school in Illinois. We spent a lot of time there, playing poker and seeing who could derive the quadratic formula the fastest while under the influence of various substances. One night at Seth's apartment, his hand on my knee turned into an unexpectedly passionate elevator ride as he escorted me downstairs to catch the bus. I was shocked at myself but gleefully shared every detail with Lisa.

The three of us often stopped midway up the mountain for a cigarette break as we climbed to our morning classes. We usually smoked Mustang, the cheap Colombian brand instead of our preferred, and expensive, Marlboro Lights. We acquired the habit of lighting three cigarettes at a time and handing them to each other. Students smoked in class and tossed their butts on the floor. It took some getting used to, but we assimilated. While waiting for the bus, several old women informed me and Lisa that only *putas* smoke in the street. Smoking in class? Check. Smoking on the street? *Ixnay.*

When we flew to the jungle for fall break, our flight was full of actual working *putas.* Seth, Lisa, and I walked into the El Dorado airport in Bogotá and bought tickets for the Amazon, to a town called Leticia which lies 300 miles south of the equator. Flying the Colombian airline Avianca in the '80s was an experience. The right side of the plane was the smoking section, and the left side was non-smoking. In other words, if you sat on the left, you weren't allowed to smoke. At any rate, we were distracted by the heavily made-up women filling most of the seats. Their raucous laughter filled the plane as they screeched and chattered across the aisle. The three of us sneaked glances at them and grinned, delighted when the women began flirting with Seth. He reddened and the women laughed louder. Upon arrival in the tiny jungle town, several men we met informed me and Lisa: *No hay mujeres como Uds. aquí.* There aren't any women like you here. At least the men could tell we weren't *putas* even if old ladies couldn't. Still, the men's longing stares were disconcerting.

The heat and humidity almost knocked us down when we deplaned into the Amazonian afternoon. The weather in Bogotá was cool and rainy year-round due to its elevation in the Andes. The jungle town of Leticia hosted a handful of hotels, bars, and restaurants. Leticia was a gateway into Colombia for coca paste from Peru and Bolivia. Colombian laboratories then processed the paste into the refined white powder that is smuggled into the United States. I was surprised to learn that many Colombians think all Americans are drug addicts. To them, drugs were an export business and only used by the lower class. Your average Colombian college student had never smoked pot, at least not the ones I met. On the other hand, whenever Seth walked down the streets of Bogotá, strangers would place drugs in his hand assuming he would buy them because he was unmistakably a gringo.

Our hotel offered a two-room suite decorated in cool tile. Ceiling fans circulated, and we threw open the shuttered windows. Seth, Lisa, and I slipped from our room to skinny dip in the murky swimming pool, the jungle inspiring us to be even more daring than normal. Gaping in surprise when another guest appeared poolside, we submerged ourselves as much as possible. The intruder's only comment was that Seth was *tan blanco como yuca*, as white as yucca – the starchy root vegetable served with most meals along with potatoes and/or rice. The inside of the yucca is startlingly white. When the stranger left the pool area, Lisa and I laughed until our stomachs ached. *Tan blanco como yuca* became a catchphrase for us, a memory spell only the three of us could summon. We'd say it when we needed a laugh in a tense moment or when we'd had enough shots of *aguardiente* to make everything hilarious.

On our second evening in the jungle, we walked to Brazil. Locals pointed us down a dirt road and off we went. The river was to our right but hidden by trees and vegetation as we headed toward the Amazon tri-border where Colombia, Brazil, and Peru meet. As daylight faded, we began to hear people in the shacks along the road speaking Portuguese instead of Spanish. We found a decrepit outdoor bar, a few wooden planks nailed together surrounded by a dozen plastic chairs. It was like an oasis in the desert, and we headed straight for it. I had my first *caipirinha*, a delicious Brazilian specialty that tastes like lemonade but is deadly. We had planned to walk to the town of Tabatinga, but we never made it beyond the bar. I may have had a second drink, Lisa and I may have danced, and monkeys may have clapped coconut shells together for all I remember.

"Time to go." Lisa and Seth hoisted me up by my arms and steered me back onto the dirt road.

"*Brigada*," I slurred in the direction of the bartender, remembering my manners. "Why don't we hedgehog back to Colombia?" I suggested to my friends.

"Do you mean hitchhike?"

"Yeah, hedgehike," I slurred.

Moments later my wish came true as we heard the rumbling of a pickup on the road behind us. I recall nothing more than a breeze on my face as our Good Samaritan drove us the two kilometers to Colombia, three American college kids in the back of his truck. What could he have thought? That corner of the Amazon was not teeming with tourists. We were the only non-Colombians we had seen. Was it kindness or curiosity that led him to stop? Either way, I was grateful for the lift.

I awoke with my limbs intertwined with Seth's, sunlight streaming in my face, and Lisa standing over us. "You look like Adam and Eve," she said when I opened one eye. I felt like Eve; an inchoate longing filled me as I lay beside Seth listening to the sounds of the rainforest. My nakedness was not yet a sin and we were still in the Garden.

Once dressed and properly awake, we walked to the center of town to catch a ferry to Benjamin Constant, a small Brazilian town where we spent the night. We drank coffee while we waited but switched to beer on the boat. It was ten in the morning, after all. Sitting on a wooden bench sipping *cerveza* from our plastic cups, we watched the muddy waters of the Amazon flow by. We disembarked in Brazil next to a herd of pigs on the riverbank. Sights like random swine no longer surprised me. After checking into a hostel, we dined on the second floor of an open-air restaurant. Lisa ordered fried fish which came with the head still attached. I was appalled since the only fish I knew came in the form of sticks.

The following morning was Sunday. Feeling contrite about my profligate ways, I convinced Lisa to slip into a local church with me. The Igreja Imaculada Conceição was an oddly modern church on a grassy plateau surrounded by palm trees. A yellow facade and square columns decorated the wide geometric body of the church. The steeple looked as though it had been stolen from a passing ship: a large parabolic sail with a metal cross on top. We hovered at the rear of the sanctuary in our inappropriate shorts and T-shirts, taking a seat in the back row. The priest, dressed in a plain brown cassock, barely drew my attention. What fascinated me were the elderly women dressed in black who filled the pews, rosaries in their gnarled hands and muttering mystical words in Latin or Portuguese. I glanced at Lisa and she, too, appeared mesmerized. I felt like an intruder in a sacred space, but I hoped the women's prayers absolved me as well. I didn't understand the words, but the Spirit spoke to me. Whatever peace we experience in this world likely comes from the fervent prayers of elderly women around the globe.

On our last day in the jungle, we offered some T-shirts to a guy to take us upriver to Peru in his canoe. Holding out my arms for balance, I stepped into the narrow boat. Once our guide started pointing out the piranhas in the water, I made sure to keep my hands, arms, and legs inside the vehicle at all times. We docked at a village where half-clothed children sold us ceviche at a wooden stand, and we danced under an open-air shelter with the locals. I possess no rhythm or grace, but I danced with joy and abandon. Our next stop was *la Isla de los Micos* – Monkey Island. We must have docked on the wrong side of the island because we were forced to trek through dense jungle to get to the monkeys. I glanced in every direction, so close to Seth I stepped on his heels repeatedly. Several men had regaled us with tales about how the world's largest anaconda was found not far from where we were. The alleged reptile was six feet around and 150 feet long. I believed every word they said. My lifelong ophidiophobia was starting to feel rational in the Amazon. I wasn't afraid of anything else in the jungle, but I was terrified I'd see a snake.

We entered a clearing and I breathed a sigh of relief. There we were greeted by a shirtless man with swept back hair known as Kapax, aka the Colombian Tarzan. Although famous for wrestling anacondas, he only showed us monkeys, thank Jesus. (Feel free to Google photos of Kapax and the anacondas.) Small squirrel monkeys swarmed us, their black and white faces standing out against their yellowish-orange fur. I was cuddling one of the cute buggers until its mate came along and nipped my ankle. I dropped that monkey faster than you can say PETA. I didn't worry about being bitten by an animal in the Amazon jungle at that moment, but a decade later when I saw the movie *Outbreak*, I had a belated panic attack as Dustin Hoffman strived to stop a deadly monkey virus that originated in the jungle.

Still holding his monkey, Seth grinned at me, and my heart skipped a beat. It was a crazy dream, standing in the Amazon with a man who made my whole body tingle with a glance. Like the characters in Gabriel García Márquez's Colombian epic *One Hundred Years of Solitude*, it was as if I had discovered ice in the jungle, and not even flying carpets could compare to the thrill. The daily danger of life in Bogotá and our reckless adventures forged a bond between us. No one else could ever understand the experience. I was trying to play it cool, assuming that "what happens in Colombia stays in Colombia" even though I knew I had caught feelings.

We returned from fall break to Uniandes in that slump of the culture shock curve I didn't learn about until decades later. On some graphs this point in time is labeled "disillusionment," but I prefer the charts that label it "hostility." We didn't realize we were following a well-established pattern of human experience; we just thought Colombia suddenly sucked. Sometimes I forget this unhappy time because overall, Colombia was one of the greatest times of my life. However, written evidence documents my hostility period.

The streets of Bogotá were full of children and adults asking for money. Many of the adults had birth defects because their mothers took thalidomide for morning sickness. Some of the street children, known as *gamines*, had been intentionally scarred so they could earn more money. Little boys lived on the streets, smoking cigarettes and drinking gasoline to keep warm and curb their hunger. Weird as it sounds, we gave these kids cigarettes and bought them Dunkin' Donuts from the store on the Séptima near the university. Sugar and nicotine were the kindnesses we could provide in that moment. You didn't see a lot of girls; many were forced into prostitution at an early age, a thought so sickening I could barely contemplate it.

A few times, the three of us visited a farm on the outskirts of Bogotá that took in *gamines*. It was run by a Catholic priest and seemed strict except for allowing the kids to smoke cigarettes.

On the bus ride to the farm, we passed a garbage dump where we could see people living in shelters built from landfill items. I could hardly believe my eyes. Human beings living in a dump? Even worse, the military regularly razed these homes to discourage people from living there without offering an alternative. In the subsequent decades, reports of death squads executing homeless men, women, and children in a "social cleansing" campaign have surfaced. Witnessing these realities first-hand in my young adulthood left an indelible mark on me. It is hard for me to live a first-world life and ignore the suffering endured by so many people on our planet when I've seen it with my own eyes. The ultra-rich spend their money on rocket ships and sports teams and super yachts when they could use it to do so much good. I question the morality of my own travel and pedicures and pricey haircuts when I've witnessed deprivation in developing countries. What if Jesus meant it when he told the rich young ruler to sell all he had and give it to the poor?

My most precious photograph from Colombia is a haunting tableau. Surrounded by five grinning gamines, I'm caught in a moment of shared joy. But the solemn face of a sixth child anchors the image. His small hands, one on each of my arms, claim me in a moment of tenderness and desperation. In his eyes, I see a yearning for something beyond the reality he knows. It's a gaze that pierces the layers of my privilege, demanding something from me that I was unable to give. He couldn't see that his soul was older than my own.

★ ★ ★

In Colombia, I learned new definitions of rich and poor. Notorious narco Pablo Escobar poured money into his home village and offered to pay Colombia's ten-billion-dollar foreign debt. He built hospitals, stadiums, soccer fields, and housing for the poor. I considered now how America's war on drugs crushed the Colombian economy. Crop eradication forced the most vulnerable communities deeper into poverty. Americans' insatiable demand for drugs drives the business. There is no supply without demand. Even the I-just-smoke-weed crowd fueled the drug trade. This was eye-opening information. The War on Drugs portrayed the Narcos as violent villains luring innocent Americans into addiction. No one considered that perhaps accountability should be shared between consumers and providers.

Despite my new understanding of wealth and poverty, I hated that my Colombian classmates considered me rich when I prided myself on my humble background. A typical conversation before class:

"*¿Tienes un carro?*"

"Well, yes, but it's used, and I paid for every penny of it from my job as a waitress."

"*¡Ganas suficiente de mesera para comprar un carro!*"

"Yes, I make good tips, but I work hard for that money. Lots of my friends' parents just buy them cars."

"*¿Y tus padres tienen piscina?*"

"Yeah, Mom and Dad have a pool, but it's a cheesy above-ground pool. Geez, it's not like it's an in-ground pool."

My Colombian friends shook their heads and smiled as I tried to convince them, "No, really, I am poor."

I clung tightly to the notion of my poverty and the corollary of my moral superiority to the wealthy. When, decades later, a little Googling confirmed that I am now one of the world's richest people, it knocked me off my block. Who knew being employed by the State of North Carolina was so lucrative? A global perspective often readjusts our views of ourselves. Whenever my husband complains about "not having any money," I remind him that we're among the wealthiest people in the world. It ticks him off.

On November 6, Lisa, Seth, and I were sitting in class when the sound of helicopters and gunfire grabbed our attention. The M-19, a Marxist guerrilla group possibly backed by Pablo Escobar, had taken over the Palacio de Justicia and was holding the Supreme Court and many others hostage. Being the intelligent young people we were, we made a beeline to see for ourselves. The Palacio was less than a mile from the university. A local TV reporter interviewed me, and I mumbled some nonsense about things like this not happening in the U.S. We hung out for a while but gave up on seeing anything exciting.

The following day, the Colombian military stormed the building, killing all the rebels, eleven Supreme Court justices, and many others, over one hundred people in all. A dozen other people were "disappeared," taken by the army and never seen again. Many human rights groups now refer to the heavy-handed response of the Colombian military as a holocaust. All I knew at the time was that the newspaper articles my mom sent me from the U.S. didn't line up with what I had seen with my own eyes. The American newspapers decried the siege by the communist terrorists while painting the Colombian army in a positive light. Colombians certainly didn't regard the military as heroes and saviors. It was an important lesson in the value of firsthand observation. Travel provides front row seats to the truth.

As if this weren't enough for my poor mother, a week later the Nevado del Ruiz volcano erupted, causing mudslides that killed 23,000 people in and around the town of Armero. Maybe you've seen the photo of Omayra Sanchez, a thirteen-year-old imprisoned in the mud and immobilized from the waist down who died after sixty agonizing hours of being trapped. The tragedy was the second deadliest volcanic incident of the twentieth century.

My mother caught the tail end of the story on the local radio news and frantically called the station for more information. The anchor fished the crumpled report out of the trash and read it to her again. I know she feared for my safety the entire time I was in Colombia. Lord, if she knew half of what went on, she would have keeled over from the shock. She had no idea how far Armero was from Bogotá (a mere hundred miles) or if it would affect me. While the mudslide didn't physically reach Bogotá, it did psychologically. Surviving a regular day in Colombia felt like an accomplishment; surviving November of 1985 shaped me permanently. The five months I lived in Bogotá as a twenty-one-year-old woman inoculated me against living fearfully. I learned that you can be laid flat by fear or stand up to it. Colombia taught me to face scary things head-on.

I could have died a dozen times, mostly from stupidity. Lisa and I walked the streets and rode the buses late at night. My new host mother (I changed families) referred to me as a *guayabo eterno* – literally an eternal guava tree, but in Colombian slang, an endless hangover. I found this mildly offensive but had no facts to counter her assertion. To further tempt fate, I accepted rides from strangers. While standing on the curb, waiting for an overcrowded bus to take me to the university, a man in a car offered me a ride. And I said yes and got in his car. I did this more than once. Surviving Colombia was a minor miracle. God watches out for fools and babies, and I was both.

Lisa deserted her host family and moved in with two gay men in an apartment close to the university. One afternoon as our trio headed to her apartment, we saw a commotion in the street. A crowd had gathered to watch a woman in the display window of a second-floor storefront who had stripped off her clothes. Eventually, the naked woman was tossed into the street.

Naturally, the three of us decided we had to help her. We guided her back to Lisa's apartment where the exhibitionist chattered nonsense for a long time. She went to the bathroom and emerged with dabs of shaving cream all over her face. In the end, we decided to take her to the police station next to Seth's apartment so they could help her. Who can imagine what the Colombian police thought when three American students brought in *una loca* demanding help? Oh, the arrogance and ignorance! They held her until we left and then let her go. We were furious and seething with self-righteousness when we saw her back on the street. Great white American savior babies.

We closed out November with a "Charlie Brown Thanksgiving," eating popcorn and toast in Seth's apartment and feeling sorry for ourselves. We listened to our three cassette tapes on repeat: *Hotel California*, *Chicago's Greatest Hits*, and *American Pie*. The storming of the Palacio de Justicia and the mudslides in Armero had rattled us, our invincibility suddenly less certain. Our impending departure for home instilled mixed feelings in all of us. In my case, the feelings were largely about Seth. Lisa and I were leaving at the end of the semester, but he was planning to stay for the entire academic year.

As soon as exams ended, we headed to Cartagena, a port city on Colombia's Caribbean coast. Lisa and I flew out the day before Seth and our friend Kyle joined us. We found a place to stay for five dollars a night a couple of blocks from the beach. Lisa and I dolled ourselves up and strolled into the five-star Hilton talking loudly to each other in animated English, flaunting our youth, our bodies, and our citizenship. We ignored the machine-gun-toting guards who attempted to question our entrance. The Organization of American States was meeting in Cartagena and many of the delegates were staying at the Hilton.

At the bar, the slightly inebriated Ambassador from the Bahamas seemed happy to pontificate to two wide-eyed

American girls. "We are willing to follow the moral lead of the United States," he told us, "But the United States must lead morally." That is something I have never forgotten.

Seth and Kyle joined us the following day and we spent our afternoons on the beach. We bought slices of sweet pineapple and watermelon from the *palenqueras*, dark women in vibrant dresses who strolled the sand balancing heavy baskets of fruit on their heads. These women descended from the Cimarrones, African slaves who escaped and formed their own outlaw society. We rode scooters into Old Cartagena and walked the walls of the castle fortress of San Felipe de Barajas. We bought last-minute souvenirs: a *pesebre* (Nativity) for my mother and llama slippers for my father; my friends stocked up on replicas of indigenous penis flutes. We had a contest to see who could bargain for the best price on a pair of sunglasses (I lost). These were glorious days, every minute magnified by the knowledge that it was coming to an end.

Late on my last night in Colombia, Seth and I were smoking cigarettes and watching the moon at the end of one of the rocky breakwaters that jut out every 200 yards along Bocagrande beach. Time tick tick ticking with only hours until I boarded a plane. I dreaded goodbye but tried to maintain my cool girl persona. Then Seth said the thing I hadn't dared hope for: he loved me and wanted to see me in the States. My cool girl persona evaporated, and I almost wept with happiness and relief.

My joy turned to confusion when I realized a man was standing behind us asking for a cigarette. How had he arrived at the end of the breakwater without us noticing? Seth stood and handed him a cigarette. Seth gave me a hand up and began to escort me back toward the beach, moving me to his far side. As we walked back toward the sand, I didn't notice the broken bottle tucked into the man's pants. He spoke to us in broken English as we walked, trying to block our path to the beach.

Seth answered in broken Spanish which made everything surreal and vaguely comical despite the aura of menace. I wasn't too freaked out because I still hadn't noticed the bulge under the man's shirt. When we made it back to the shore, Seth pointed in the direction of our hotel and urged me to "Run!" I hesitated for a minute, but then ran without stopping until I reached the hostel.

I paced and fretted until Seth arrived ten minutes later. Relief coursed through me. Seth told me the man wanted the cheap pearl ring I was wearing. Once I was gone, there was nothing to steal. We laughed and joked about how this must have been his first robbery attempt. I'd survived five months in Bogotá without incident only to face my first bad actor hours before departure. At the airport, I sobbed as Lisa and I boarded the plane to Miami, only vaguely aware of the other passengers' curious looks. I wasn't only distraught about leaving Seth; the terrible, magical challenge of Colombia was over. I was returning to a familiar life, one that didn't challenge or teach me daily.

★ ★ ★

When I arrive home, the reverse culture shock is worse than the original culture shock. The first time I drive my car, a bird flies into the grill of my car, and I laugh. A piece of my American optimism has been reshaped into fatalism. Death is not as foreign or frightening as it was before. I greet my old friends and move to kiss them on both cheeks as has become my custom. They step back, startled and confused. I have a tan in December and have lost twenty pounds. People look at me differently though I don't know if it's due to internal or external changes. All conversations seem petty and shallow and vain, and the ease of getting through a day leaves me feeling unaccomplished and depressed. I miss Seth. I sell the beautiful emerald ring I bought in a private store guarded by men with machine guns because I feel desperate for money. In time, I become an American again, but with a piece of my soul forever altered. I've seen how other people live. I've shared unforgettable adventures with a new lover and new friends. I've lived boldly and unsheltered in the world. I know that who I thought I was is not all I'm going to be.

José Arcadio Buendía, the patriarch in *One Hundred Years of Solitude,* develops an obsession with alchemy after Melquíades introduces him to the practice. Alchemists seek not only to turn base materials into gold but also to answer fundamental philosophical questions and to redeem the soul. The first law of alchemy is that of equivalent exchange: to obtain or create something, something of equal value must be lost or destroyed. I had to lose some of myself to become the person Colombia shaped me into being. It was a lesson I'd learn over and over as I became something of an alchemist myself.

COSTA RICA: PURA VIDA

Our plane circled San José for a long time. Lightning crack-led outside the portholes; thunderstorms were preventing our landing. The students in the window seats pressed their faces against the rain-streaked glass, mesmerized. They all seemed okay, even the ones flying for the first time. The seat belt sign was on, so I couldn't check on all sixteen of them, but I didn't hear any cries of distress or anyone screaming my name. Brooks, one of my favorite students, clapped her hands in excitement. My mom had always hoped I'd become a missionary, but rather than bringing Christ to the world, I was taking students into it. As we continued our flight pattern above the Mineta airport, I thought about my first flight, the day the world opened before me.

Our class had been on a one-day field trip to our nation's capital. My parents got up before dawn to drive me to the Winston-Salem airport where my class milled around excitedly before boarding a Piedmont airline plane, piloted by our teach-er's husband. My body tingled with excitement as the engines started and we barreled down the runway. The moment we left the ground was a miracle akin to my baptism at age 7, rising and inhaling sweet air, reborn. As we rose higher, I marveled at the early morning light illuminating the clouds, which floated like icebergs on a transparent sea. *This must be heaven*, I thought.

That day in DC is a blur, endless traipsing through the city with stops to view towering monuments, real dinosaur bones, and a glittering blue diamond. We stood at the feet of marble presidents we had studied and ate our bag lunches on the steps of the Capitol. We flew home the same evening, arriving back at the Winston-Salem airport exhausted and overwhelmed. Still glowing like a cloud backlit by the sun, I greeted my parents, feeling immensely sophisticated. I had traveled through space and time. Famous landmarks were now part of my memory and not just pictures in a book. History and government had come alive for me. I had seen the world from above and my perspective had shifted. My spark of natural curiosity had been stoked into a bonfire. It was my first awakening to the power of travel, but I never imagined it would become my life's mission to spread its transformational impact with others.

Now I was leading a group of community college students to Costa Rica, teaching them how to leave the world behind and leap into the unknown. It was a daunting responsibility. In the sixteen years since Colombia, I had accumulated many markers on my life map: a master's degree in Spanish literature, a husband named Craig, a furry black dog with tan eyebrows, a mortgage on a blue farmhouse, a gloriously nerdy son, a funny and sassy daughter, and a full-time teaching position. While relieved to have my life settled, my wanderlust was not sated. I'd squeezed in a few more trips abroad since Colombia: a honeymoon in London where I was deathly ill with the flu, a second honeymoon in Mexico when Playa del Carmen was still a charming fishing village, and a month-long stint in Madrid working as a technical translator for Ma Bell. I used the birth of my son as an excuse to leave the corporate world and return to academia, even though the excessive stress and workload might not have fazed me had management not been so horrendous. Maybe my feminist card should be revoked for using my baby as an excuse to give up 80-hour work weeks, but I've never regretted the decision. Parenting is its own foray into a brave new world.

I thought about my kids as we continued to circle the Costa Rican capital, city lights beckoning below. At almost four and seven, Anna and Daniel were old enough to understand that I was going away for ten days and that I would be back. I missed them but was also happy for a little break and secretly hoped everyone would appreciate me a little more when I returned. I did worry about being a bad mother, but I *always* worry about being a bad mother, so that was nothing new. Motherhood is such a huge responsibility; I am always floored when a woman says she's a good mother. Who could possibly make such a claim when every maternal moment is fraught with the peril of screwing up your kids' lives forever? Now adults, my children say I was a fairly good mother except for "being extra," "thinking I'm funny when I'm not," and "loving them a little too much sometimes." At least my Costa Rica excursion didn't cause them irreparable psychological damage, though Anna does have a wee fear of abandonment. Okay, probably my fault. She also has a talent for writing personal notes, a love for travel, and an intolerance for injustice. Hopefully, also my fault.

I knew the kids would be fine with Craig even if they didn't brush their teeth twice daily in my absence. They would certainly not go hungry; Craig has been our primary cook since the early days of our marriage. My husband is a steady and faithful partner and father. He can be cranky at times, but his insides are pure marshmallow. He grows tomatoes to take to the people on his Meals-on-Wheels route and stops to help turtles cross the road. He makes up love songs to me, including the classic "Take the Croutons from your Hair." I knew Craig even before I went to Colombia; he was a regular at the restaurant I'd worked at since high school. He lived in the neighborhood and worked down the street as the technical director of the newly revitalized performing arts theater. Seven years older than me, he was already balding but had a cool mustache and nice green eyes.

He and his friends were engaging and funny – we presented them with greatly reduced bills, and they tipped us generously in return, though their gratuities often included stage whispered "tips" for horse betting: *Swordfish in the third.* Luckily, they included cash, too. On several occasions over the years, Craig and I had gone on friendly dates with the understanding I had a serious boyfriend in the Coast Guard or Illinois or wherever. Finally, the timing was right. He asked me out again a couple of months after Seth and I broke up.

The relationship with Seth had lasted through graduate school in Illinois, but frigid temperatures and cornfields did not provide the same otherworldly backdrop as Colombia. I longed for Seth throughout our relationship, even the year we shared a house and a bed. Though I was with him in every tangible way, he was always distant from me. A prodigious weed-smoker, Seth refused to feel his feelings even more adamantly than I did. Maybe my fierce desire for him was simply a result of his refusal to be emotionally available – desperation for the thing I couldn't have. There's nothing more desirable than forbidden fruit. When I felt him growing even more distant, I pressured him to marry me, but he declined. My heart was broken again, but this time the pain was less acute, a chronic ache versus a stabbing pain. I rarely think about the high school boyfriend who broke my heart the first time, but to my dismay, Seth haunts my sleep to this day. The dreams are pleasant, but I'm pissed off when I wake up and realize that Seth is still a major player in my sub-conscious all these decades later. Maybe it's not him I miss, but the thrill of a relationship forged in precariousness and novelty.

My first post-Seth date with Craig was an afternoon hockey game for the Olympic trials. I had fond memories of hockey from my childhood when my dad took me to his moonlighting job at the coliseum and I cheered on the Winston-Salem Polar Twins with bloodthirsty gusto. Wrestling matches, however, had been my favorite event at the coliseum. I adored watching the Mighty Igor – a fat, hairy, congenial mess of a man in a unitard. Watching a Polish wrestler beat bad guys over the head with his kielbasa was the pinnacle of an international cultural event in my childhood. The hockey game with Craig was fun, though I later learned he took a different girl to the evening game. I can't really blame him for hedging his bets where I was concerned.

After a mere year of dating, Craig and I married on New Year's Eve 1989. Our London honeymoon was his first international trip, and while he enjoyed England once we got there (despite his sickly bride), he hated flying. I've spent years molding Craig into a traveler. A homebody by nature, he tends to worry about everything that could go wrong. While he believes I am book smart, he says I have the common sense God gave a sack of hammers. He's always supported my adventures, accepting early on that I was "going to do what I wanted anyway." Over the years, he's learned that the physical drudgery of travel is almost always worth it. Everything got easier when our missionary friend who runs an orphanage in Kenya taught me how to drug him in preparation for international flights. There's no shame in managing anxiety with medication. Still, I think he was relieved when our kids were born, assuming that having children would tether me to our home. It did, for a while.

I left corporate America for academia after the birth of our son, Daniel. When I accepted the position of Spanish Instructor in 1994, I was completely ignorant about community colleges. I brought the same biases and misunderstandings that many people have. I had no idea that over a third of all college students in the U.S. attend a community college. I didn't understand that community colleges were created to democratize higher education, giving opportunities to farm workers and other rural students who couldn't go away to college. It had not occurred to me that the racial and economic diversity of community college students far exceeded that of universities. Community college faculty are not expected to do research or publish, but they have a far heavier teaching load than university professors. They're also expected to care about their students and help them succeed.

Initially, I was frustrated by some students' lack of preparedness even though I knew they hadn't been afforded the same educational opportunities that I'd had. Though my family was working class, my sister and I had been selected for the county's highly gifted program and spent our formative years studying alongside wealthy classmates. Most of my students at the community college did not come from affluent families, yet I complained a lot about what they didn't know during my first years of teaching. Had they not learned anything in twelve years of school?

Then I had an epiphany.

While chatting with a young woman at my church who was heading off to a university, it dawned on me: She will thrive wherever she goes. She already possesses the skills and knowledge to be successful and no major obstacles stand in her way. Most community college students have many hurdles, and their success is not guaranteed. I have a real influence on whether my students succeed. If they don't learn something about the world from me, there's a chance they'll never learn it. When I realized that it was at a community college where I could make the biggest difference in students' lives, it changed everything.

For the first few years, I was happy to teach and advise the Spanish Club and pick up my kids from the campus daycare as soon as I could. Eventually, the French instructor talked me into joining her campaign to convince the administration to let us take students abroad. The college president at the time had a low tolerance for risk and didn't understand the value of travel for our students. Community colleges focus on the local. We had to convince him that in the new millennium local *is* global. As technology and globalization have brought the world closer together, all students need to have a global perspective. No one is truly educated if they are clueless about the 96 percent of the world's population that live outside the U.S. We finally received permission to plan short faculty-led study abroad programs. In 2000, the French instructor took a group to Paris, and I began planning a 2001 trip to Costa Rica.

I chose Costa Rica because it was a Spanish-speaking country I had never visited and a destination with outdoor activities that would appeal to college students. I offered the second free chaperone spot to Sarah, a beautiful young English instructor at the college who shared my smoking habit and thereby qualified as the ideal roommate. Tall and willowy with long dark hair courtesy of her Greek and Native American ancestry, Sarah was surely the object of many students' desires. I began to question my decision to offer her the spot when Sarah mentioned that she would go topless on the beach if we went somewhere it was allowed.

"You would not," I said, shocked.

"Sure, I would."

"In front of students?"

"Sure."

"You would not," I informed her. I was years away from running the college's international education program, but this provided me with my first foray into setting faculty expectations. It's a big mistake to assume people have the same ideas as you do about what behavior is appropriate. To be fair, I made many choices in Costa Rica that would have appalled me later in my career, mainly alcohol related. These include letting Sarah talk one-on-one with an intoxicated male student in his hotel room about his suicidal ideations, drinking freely with students at the beach bar, and worst of all, providing students with shots of *guaro* (Costa Rica's sugarcane-based liquor) from a bottle in my room. What was I thinking?

Another concern about Sarah was that when I first asked her to be a co-leader on the program, she confused Costa Rica with Cambodia. Americans tend to be woefully ignorant of geography and while I no longer expect students to have any familiarity with a world map, I had different expectations for faculty. That turned out to be a faulty assumption. Let's just say that many of the instructors at the rural community college would not crush the World Geography category on Jeopardy. I made it part of my mission to incorporate geography education into everything I did at my job. How can you understand yourself if you have no concept of your place in the world?

In case you don't know, Costa Rica is in Central America, between Nicaragua and Panama. Another fun fact is that Central America is a subregion of *North* America. Costa Rica is famous for not having an army. In 1987, their President, Óscar Arias, won the Nobel Peace Prize for his plan to end the civil wars devastating other countries in the region. Known for eco-tourism, the small nation contains five percent of the world's biodiversity. They generate ninety-nine percent of their electricity with renewable energy sources. *Ticos*, as they call themselves, rank as the happiest people in the Western Hemisphere. The unofficial national slogan is *pura vida* which means *pure life* but serves not only as a greeting but as a general reflection of the optimistic nature of the culture. Perhaps a better translation would be, "It's all good." *Pura vida* is the answer to almost any question you can ask a *tico*.

Most of the students in our group were traditionally aged college students, except for Wendy, Eszter, and Eszter's son. Wendy was an older blonde student in my Spanish class from rural Virginia. Eszter was a Hungarian nursing student who barraged me with endless questions about the trip for months before departure. She was loud and rude, without any self-awareness. The other students found her insufferable and felt sorry for her nine-year-old son. As I was to learn, there's always one problem student on every study abroad program, the person who aggravates the rest of the group, the one you wouldn't cry about if they accidentally fell into a volcano even though it would generate a lot of paperwork and damage the reputation of the program. I consider it one of my less appealing job duties to spend time with this person and give the rest of the group a break when possible. I try to sneak in a few teachable moments about cultural competence. I view myself as an alchemist, mixing science and magic with travel to transform students from 'ugly Americans' into golden examples of intercultural sensitivity. Well, maybe not golden examples, but improved.

Truthfully, instilling cultural competence was not top of mind once our plane finally landed in San José. I couldn't wait to get to the hotel and hit the sack. After collecting our luggage from baggage claim, we were met by Di, our not-particularly friendly tour director. A bus whisked us away through the dark streets of the city to a generic hotel downtown. Once room keys were distributed, I gave my students orders to go straight to bed and to not leave the hotel. The bus was leaving early the next morning for a day filled with pueblos, volcanoes, and waterfalls. I didn't want my rural kiddos out partying in a big city where they didn't speak the language. I had taught Spanish to most of them and could attest that their *español* was *no bueno*.

We spent most of our days on the bus, traveling from hot springs to rainforests to beaches. Sloths, monkeys, coatimundi, toucans, and crocodiles dotted the landscapes. Brooks held a scarlet snake at the serpentarium near Montevideo. I shrank back in fear as a viper lunged at us from its enclosure, leaving venom dripping on the glass. While hiking deep in the rainforest, the sky opened and soaked us through, leaving the bus smelling like a load of laundry left in the washer too long for the rest of our journey. But even unpleasant shared experiences contribute to group bonding.

One of the worst experiences of my life was ziplining in Costa Rica, though I tried to hide my trauma from the group. Brooks thought I was acting bitchy because I was terrified. That was only half of it: I was terrified *and* humiliated. My students didn't know that the young guides who strapped me into my harness were talking in Spanish about my weight. It didn't occur to the young *ticos* that an American group leader might be fluent in Spanish. Sometimes it's an advantage to speak a language that no one knows you speak; on this occasion it sucked. I started to say something in Spanish so they would stop commenting about my size but decided it would just make everything worse.

A combination of fear and shame washed over me. I was completely dysregulated as we climbed a rope ladder one hundred feet up the inside of a hollow Ficus tree. I felt like a condemned prisoner being marched to the firing squad, but it didn't cross my mind to back out. I am nothing, if not committed. If you want to guarantee that I do something, tell me that I can't or shouldn't.

When we reached the vertiginous top of the tree, a few of us at a time crowded onto the tiny wooden platform. Far in the distance, I could make out the figure of another guide on the destination platform. Fearing my bulk would send me hurtling down the line, knocking the guide off the platform into the forest below, I braked hard halfway across. I dangled over the canopy of the cloud forest, worrying my weight would snap the line. I was forced to turn around and pull myself hand over hand to the small wooden square. This happened on each of the lines. When we reached the last platform, I learned I had to rappel down the rope ten stories to the ground. I have never been athletic or coordinated, and this was a final humiliation. The students took pictures of me (i.e., my butt) on the way down, unaware of my psychological crisis. I ended up displaying one of those photos in my scrapbook. It reminds me that I can do hard things even when people doubt me. Especially when people doubt me. Facing fear head on diminishes its power.

My weight has been the struggle of my life, and the struggle is real. My mom recently gave me a stack of my old school papers including one from third grade titled "About Me." We were instructed to answer a variety of prompts about our likes and dislikes.

"What do you wish you were better at?" one of the questions on the paper read.

"Losing weight," answered eight-year-old me.

I wasn't chubby as a baby or preschooler, but I'd gotten mildly plump by third grade. Even at age eight, I knew that being overweight was a sin – a moral fault, a shameful failure, evidence of a weak will. I was lazy, gluttonous, undisciplined. My battle with food began when I was in utero. For years, Mom proudly told the story about how she didn't gain any weight during her pregnancy with me. My dad was in the Air Force and the military doctor had allegedly lost a pregnant woman to obesity. Since my mother was fifteen pounds overweight, the traumatized doc put her on a strict diet. She was ordered to eat a lot of liver and not much else. Mom recounts hungrily sniffing the mustard as she made my father's lunch each day. It was all worth it when she pranced home from the hospital in her tiny yellow corduroy skirt set. It took me more than five decades to realize this wasn't a story to be proud of, even though she still is. I don't blame her—she was twenty years old and following doctor's orders. I weighed exactly seven pounds at birth; at least I was at an ideal weight at one point in my life.

By the last day in Costa Rica, the shame and horror of ziplining had faded a bit. I am an expert in compartmentalization, and

I had shoved the incident into a drawer in the back of my psyche. I was enjoying the time with my students. We were staying at a beach resort in Punta Leona and spent our evening dancing and drinking tropical beverages on a thatched roof patio. Costa Rican calypso music blared from the speakers. *Pura vida.*

"Hey, LaVenture," called one of the boys across the bar. "I guess we can confess now."

I instantly sobered up. "Confess to what?"

"The night we arrived in San José? Four of us went to a strip club."

I was pissed. Not only did they ignore my explicit instructions not to leave the hotel, but they went to a freaking strip club. I don't judge the dancers, but I do judge men who pay to lust after the bodies of women they don't know. The students looked worried, fearing their confession had been a mistake. As I mulled over my response, the first night in Costa Rica seemed so long ago. Time passes differently when you're in another country. What could I do about it now?

"Assholes," I finally said. They grinned and let out their breath. That's one of the things I love about leading study abroad. I could never call my students assholes on campus, but in another country, the student-teacher relationship takes on a new shape. They were delighted that I called them assholes. There are still boundaries, but they loosen up considerably. In a foreign setting, an instructor begins to take on human form in the eyes of her students. I could never get over my own children's shock over seeing their teachers in the grocery store.

"*Oh my gosh*, it's Mrs. Murphy," one of them would cry. "What's she doing at Food Lion?'

You'd think they'd seen an alien.

"I'm a teacher," I'd remind them.

"Yeah, but that's different."

Studying abroad affords students the opportunity to dis-covery the humanity of others, including their instructors and classmates. It was clear my students had been changed by the experience even given the short duration of the program. Not only did they know more about Costa Rica and biological diver-sity, but they were also more confident, more curious about other cultures, more open to the idea that "different" is not a synonym for "bad." They lost some of their fear of speaking Spanish and formed lasting friendships with others in the group. Glad they had spent the time and money, they all wanted to travel again. The positive changes I witnessed convinced me that travel is the best teacher. One of the young men wrote the fol-lowing in my Costa Rica scrapbook:

"Experiences like these are rare to some lives. The fact remains that as incredible as the trip and atmosphere was, it was you and our group experiencing it together that made it so much more precious. I can never verbalize the appreciation I have for you. I can only say thank you for your priceless gift."

I had come full circle from Colombia, from studying abroad to leading a study abroad program. In just the ten days since our plane circled the San José airport, the lives of sixteen people had been altered by an international travel experience. My new mission was clear: take as many students abroad as I possibly could. Lives were waiting to be transformed, and I could make that happen.

SPAIN AND MOROCCO - COEXIST

My heart pounded as I strolled through the Alcázar in Sevilla, deep in the heart of Andalucía, the southern-most region of Spain. It wasn't because of the Moorish palace's amazing architecture, lush gardens, or rich history, but because Orlando Bloom had just finished filming *Kingdom of Heaven* there. Strolling through the compound and gardens, I tingled at the thought that my "boyfriend" had been in this very spot so recently. I imagined him lounging on a chaise under a mosaic tile ceiling while I fed him grapes, making eyes at him from behind my veil and trying not to dig my *I Dream of Jeannie* costume out of my crack. It had been three years since I was first smitten with Orlando in *The Fellowship of the Ring*. Now my obsession was reaching its apex and would sustain itself at a near-psychotic level for several more years.

The final film in *The Lord of the Rings* trilogy premiered six months earlier. Orlando plays Legolas, an ancient-but-super-hot Sindarin elf of the Woodland Realm. With flowing blond locks, an eagle eye, incredible archery skills, and the ability to walk on top of snow, Legolas is not your Santa's elf. I was slightly ashamed of my obsession, mainly because Orlando was in his mid-twenties and I was in my late thirties. Plus, being infatu-ated with an elf is a bit embarrassing, even though Legolas is a *warrior* elf. Fifteen years into my marriage and ten years into motherhood and my community college career, a little fantasy went a long way. A fictional affair with an elf seemed a relatively harmless expression of mid-life angst. There was nothing *wrong* with my life, but something felt missing. I filled the cracks with elven fantasy.

The world had changed in the three years since I took students to Costa Rica. The events of 9/11 had altered everything. There were serious concerns about international travel. The Spain program I selected for my second faculty-led study abroad program almost literally derailed two months before our departure date. On my fortieth birthday, bombs exploded on four commuter trains in Madrid, killing 191 people and injuring two thousand. I watched the news from my hotel in Charleston, South Carolina, where Craig, the kids, and I were celebrating my big day with a visit to my natal city. I sat there shell-shocked, the horror of turning forty paling in the face of a real tragedy. Originally thought to be the work of Basque separatists, the explosions were eventually traced to Moroccan jihadists inspired by Al Qaeda.

Three of the bombs exploded in the Atocha train station, directly across the street from the hotel in which we were booked to stay upon arrival. Details of the tragedy mixed in my mind with worry about the impact on the study abroad program. I found it difficult to enjoy the birthday bash with my family. I couldn't get the attack and its implications out of my mind. To go or not to go? That was the question.

As a risk-taker, my inclination was to move full steam ahead. I don't like the idea of letting terrorists succeed in instilling terror. I may feel the fear, but my fight-or-flight response is almost always to fight. (I'm an Enneagram 8, if that means anything to you.) Plus, Madrid was likely one of the safer places to be in Europe since it was unlikely that terrorists would strike in the same spot, and security would be high. I was relieved when the college administrators granted permission to go ahead with the program. For once I was happy that none of my students paid attention to the news. No one dropped out, and we landed in Madrid two months later.

My roommate on the trip was Brooks, my favorite student from Costa Rica. Since graduating with her associate's degree, we'd become close friends. When not in class working on her bachelor's degree, she babysat my kids or came over to watch movies after they'd gone to bed while my husband brought us glasses of wine. It was a bizarre relationship because we didn't fit any mold. Was I still her teacher? A second mother? Or just friends? My kids loved her, and she was part of our family. She taught Daniel to swim and dyed Easter eggs with Anna. Craig liked her, too. Her sense of humor and brilliant smile brought joy to all our lives. Frankly, I adored her. She also filled those little cracks of malaise in me.

In Spain, distance was growing between us because I disapproved of her relationship with the person she was dating. In retrospect, I was completely wrong. They have been happily married for many years. At the time I was judgy and inflexible, and my attitude made me feel terrible, but I had yet to reach a place where I stopped trying to control the lives of the people I love. (Not completely there yet, but I'm working on it.) Maybe I was simply trying not to lose Brooks, but I pushed her away in the process of trying to hold onto her. It broke my heart, but I was incapable of changing my thinking at the time. I've regretted it ever since.

The strain between us was uncomfortable, but I was cheered when we visited the famous Mezquita of Córdoba. A pagan temple originally stood on the site, but invading Visigoths converted it to a Christian church in 572. When the Moors arrived from North Africa in 711, they converted it to a mosque. Eventually converted back to a Catholic cathedral, most people still refer to it as the Great Mosque due to its dazzling architecture. The huge column-filled prayer hall reminds me of a scene from *The*

Fellowship of the Ring when the fellowship is forced to pass through the Mines of Moria on their quest to destroy the One Ring. The nine emerge from subterranean tunnels into a great hall with a seemingly infinite number of arched columns. Standing in the Mosque of Córdoba, imagining the iconic arches swarming with orcs, I slipped back into my fantasy world where Legolas would sling arrows at all my problems and make clear what was pure and noble and true. My mental fan fiction was a comfort to me. Just like novels, my own fantasies provided me with an escape from the daily grind.

From Córdoba, we headed southwest to Seville, where I walked in Orlando's literal footprints at the Alcázar where filming of *Kingdom of Heaven* had ended only a month before. Classical concerts take place in the gardens on summer evenings, and though we were there in the afternoon, the plants and water and architecture created a melody of their own. From the palace, our group ambled through the Jewish quarter and arrived at the Seville Cathedral, the largest Gothic church in the world. Taught to be suspicious of Catholicism by my Southern Baptist upbringing, I held the excesses of the Roman Church in contempt and scorned the ornate cathedrals built on the backs of the poor. But I was profoundly moved in the Seville Cathedral, by the soaring nave, beautiful paintings, and eighty side chapels. The main altarpiece rises high, with scenes from the Old Testament and the lives of the saints gilded in gold. I sat in the pew trying to imagine being a parishioner 500 years ago when odds were I couldn't read, and the altarpiece was my only source of stories. The sacred was vivid and alive in the cavernous space. Tears stained my cheeks. I've felt the presence of God in my life since I was small, and He won't go away, even when I'd prefer for Him to make Himself scarce. The cathedral was designed to illustrate the vastness of God, but I was still bound by the smallness of my beliefs.

I glanced up and noticed a group of my students standing next to the tomb of Christopher Columbus. History regarded Columbus as a hero for centuries, but these days he is viewed by many as a villain, responsible for the genocide of native peoples. A man who was allegedly guided by his faith behaved in ways that today seem blatantly evil. Still, there's no denying that he changed the world irrevocably. It's a lightbulb moment when students realize for the first time that historical events have directly shaped their lives. These are the moments I live for. As one student wrote: "Learning and experiencing things in person is so different and life changing. Being able to stand exactly where historical events took place is completely different from seeing it in a photograph or reading about it."

I witness these lightbulb moments on every study abroad program. They feed my passion for taking students abroad. I need them to balance out the dark moments that also happen on every trip. These dreary moments are often caused by people from other groups. Colleges are often combined on these tours, and in Spain, we were cursed with a group of frat boys from a university an hour away from us. Their faculty leader was an accounting professor who was so drunk the whole time that his students often had to help him on and off the bus. He was traveling with his eighteen-year-old daughter, and my heart went out to her.

Around two in the morning during our night in Seville, I heard shouting coming from the hotel lobby. Our rooms lined an open interior courtyard, and from the third floor I could see that the ruckus was being caused by a few of the sterling citizens from the other group. Stepping to the railing, I asked them to quiet down in a stern but not unkind manner. They responded with a barrage of cursing and insults. My blood boiled. At this point, several doors on the third floor flew open, and my students began to shout at the other students for cussing me out. It made me happy that my students came to my rescue, but I was rattled by the behavior of the other group. Talk about assholes. Brooks tried to convince me to ignore them, but I tossed and turned thinking about the joy of the next day's long bus ride with them.

From Seville, we zigzagged back east to Granada where we toured the Alhambra, an Islamic fortress and palace first built in 889 and renovated in the mid-thirteenth century. When Ferdinand and Isabella finally drove the last of the Moors from Spain in 1492, this became the seat of their Royal Court. It was here that Columbus petitioned the Catholic Monarchs to fund his expedition to India. Later we visited the Royal Chapel, where the lavish burial monuments of Ferdinand and Isabella are carved in Carrara marble. More interestingly, a small staircase leads under the tombs to a small crypt. Here the actual remains of the Spanish Monarchs lie in austere coffins. Four plain lead boxes house Ferdinand and Isabella, their daughter Juana la Loca, and her husband Felipe el Hermoso. A box of bones is all that's left of two of history's most influential figures. Death is indeed the great equalizer, and it comes for all of us. At the time, I didn't know Death would be making a direct run at me in a little over a decade. We know it's inevitable, but we're always surprised when *la muerte* crooks its finger in our direction.

Our final stop was Marbella, a beach town on the Costa del Sol. I dipped my feet in the Mediterranean as soon as we arrived, but I had no interest in a beach day. I was stoked for the optional excursion the following day: taking a ferry across the Strait of Gibraltar to Morocco. Traveling to Africa had been on the top of my bucket list for a long time. Half of our group opted to stay behind, but the fun people woke before dawn and took the bus to Algeciras to catch the ferry. Sadly, our scheduled crossing was canceled because the sea was too rough. Our options were 1) wait and see if the waves calmed down for the next scheduled crossing or 2) go back to the beach. The students voted for the beach. I pouted, cajoled, and gave a wee inspirational speech channeling my inner Aragorn. It worked: They agreed to wait. As we chugged past the Rock of Gibraltar, I could only think how weird it was to see a Prudential ad in real life.

We landed in Ceuta, a Spanish territory on the African continent, where we found our bus and met our guide, Abdul.

"Just call me Michael Douglas," he informed us by way of introduction, claiming he looked just like the "famous American movie star." On this day, another of my unconscious biases was revealed to me: I was surprised to learn that Muslims had a sense of humor. "Michael Douglas" was hilarious, possibly the funniest tour guide I ever had. After crossing the border into Morocco, we stopped by the side of the road where we got to ride a camel long enough to snap a photo. In Tétouan, the medina burst with vibrant colors—saffron, scarlet, brilliant blue. The markets teemed with life, from the snake charmer's hypnotic cobra to the bustling stalls of spices and carcasses. The notes from a *pungi*, a flute-like instrument made from a gourd, filled the square as a snake rose from a basket seemingly in time to the music. The sights and sounds created a sensory overload reminding me how vast and varied the world can be.

Our lunch consisted of chicken and rice bathed in rich spices. Our drink arrived in a glass bottle, familiar in every way except for the lettering: الكوكاكولا – the Arabic spelling of Coca-Cola. A mustached man dressed in embroidered red silk entered the room, balancing a tray of lit candles on his head. Performing an energetic dance, he slid across the floor without quenching a flame, while the students applauded. Following lunch, we went carpet shopping. Sitting on benches around the periphery of a large room, we learned about handmade rugs. With bold colors and geometric patterns, each design tells the story of a nomadic journey. Every thread adds to the story, creating a complex and beautiful tapestry. We learned about the symbols and motifs woven into the textiles – from eyes and hands to ward off the evil eye to a lizard representing the soul's search for light.

Our last stop was a traditional Moroccan "pharmacy" which bore no resemblance to a CVS. Again, we sat on wooden benches in a small shop filled with shelves of jars containing herbs and potions, many as colorful as the spices we saw in the market. The pharmacist described the healing powers of the oils and seeds and creams. I volunteered when they offered a neck massage and a handsome young man with bad teeth began to work the knots out. I didn't buy any love potions or wrinkle cream, but I did get some saffron for an incredibly low price. Leaving the shop, we heard the haunting and beautiful call to prayer echoing through the streets. The Arabic words were not decipherable, but the voice was warm and inviting. As we walked back to our bus, we passed an open doorway where men were kneeling in reverent supplication.

This naturally turned my thoughts back to Orlando Bloom. *Kingdom of Heaven*, the movie he filmed in Spain and Morocco, was a twelfth-century epic about the Crusades. Having just spent a wonderful day in a Muslim country enjoying tremendous hospitality, the heightened worldwide tensions between Christians and Muslims lay heavy on my heart. While Christians, Jews, and Muslims lived somewhat peacefully in Spain for centuries, eventually the *cristianos* drove out the others. I wondered dejectedly what I could do to influence people away from fear and hatred and toward mutual understanding. Glancing ahead, I noticed my students joking and laughing with "Michael Douglas." I smiled as I realized I was doing just that, one student at a time.

Travel is more than a chance to explore unfamiliar places; it is also about considering ideas that challenge our long-held beliefs. Being able to view things from multiple perspectives is key to true understanding. Just like the blind men describing various parts of an elephant, I was starting to realize that my perceptions were incomplete. At the ripe old age of forty I still had a long way to grow in wisdom and understanding. My heart was broken about my inability to accept Brooks' choice, but a broken heart is an open heart. I wasn't ready to give up all of my biases, but seeds had been planted in the cracks.

MÉXICO AND THE BRITISH
ISLES: STALKING BONO

Like travel, music is a source of transformational magic.
Ditties, ballads, arias, hymns, carols, chants, jingles, sym-
phonies, show tunes, sea shanties, psalms, anthems, rebel songs.
Music puts babies to sleep, inspires religious ecstasy, and fuels
activism. Specific songs can enable time travel, mend a broken
heart, inspire dancing, or comfort the mourning. From lullabies
to dirges, music is the universal language. Every human culture
makes music. Everybody sings. In ancient Greece, they believed
that the movement of celestial bodies created *musica universalis*,
the inaudible music of the spheres felt by every soul.

The Irish rock band U2 provides the soundtrack for my life;
their music is another tool for caulking up the holes in my soul.
In October 1987 in Champaign, Illinois, where I was a grad student, my friend Angie entered the ticket lottery for The Joshua
Tree Tour. She scored twelfth-row seats, so I tagged along even
though I felt *meh* about the lads from Dublin. I entered U of
I's Assembly Hall as an observer and left as a true believer.
A sweaty, long-haired Bono sang straight into my soul like a
preacher stealin' hearts in a travelin' show. Most people don't
believe me when I say my love for Bono is nonsexual, but it's
true. I admire him for his talent and intelligence, his steady
faith, his long marriage to his high school sweetheart, his commitment to his bandmates, and his work on behalf of the world's

poor. I think of Bono and me as besties who don't know each other.

Almost two decades after first seeing U2 in concert, I found myself in Monterrey, Mexico, nursing a case of strep throat with a margarita while a fake Bono wailed in an open-air restaurant. My friend Susan and I had planned this madcap adventure after seeing the band play in Charlotte a few months previously. Eighteen years my senior, Susan's eccentricity is irrepressible. She likes sparkly shoes, patting strangers on the head, and performing ballet leaps in parking lots. Last summer, she spent an hour swimming in her neighbor's beach house pool by accident. We share a love of books, film, travel, food, wine, and Jesus. We squabble over baptism and Calvinism and praying for dead people. We also argue over whether rhubarb is disgusting (it is), what color mauve is (purple), and if Peter Falk is more attractive than Chris Hemsworth (he is not).

Susan had never been to a rock concert. She was a military brat with a high-ranking father whose strict insistence on perfection had made her rebel in some ways, but not in the rock-and-roll way. I introduced her to U2, and she and her husband Gene saw the band play in Charlotte in December 2005, a few months before our trip to Mexico. They had seats for the show while Craig and I stood on the floor in front of the stage. U2 shows are spiritual experiences, and like me at my first show, Susan was converted.

Hoping to get Bono's autograph at the Charlotte show, Craig and I had arrived early so I could stand outside the stage door in the cold drizzle. Our General Admission tickets meant we'd be queueing to stand in front of the stage come showtime. Craig held our place in line inside so we could get a good spot when the doors opened. Huddling outside in the chilly rain with a dozen other extreme fans, I was thrilled when a black sedan pulled in. A man emerged from the car, but it wasn't Bono.

"It's Brian!" the crowd announced.

We groaned when Bono's head of security informed us that the singer wasn't going to be able to stop because he was having dinner backstage with Jesse Helms. We didn't disperse. Fifteen minutes later another black sedan appeared. The tinted window rolled down and there was *himself* (as the Irish say), wearing a cowboy hat and waving. He apologized for not having time to stop. Then the tinted window slid up and the car entered the building.

It was particularly vexing to be thwarted by Jesse Helms. I had long despised the ultra-conservative politician from North Carolina known as "Senator No." Yet, I admired Bono's approach with him. Instead of writing off Helms as an obvious opponent to providing aid to fight global poverty and disease, Bono convinced Helms to support AIDS relief in Africa. He listened to Helms and then pointed out that Helms' belief system required him to help the sick and the poor. While some criticized Bono for his friendship with Helms, now I try to emulate it. I don't reject people who disagree with me; I want to convince them to change their minds. I also try to listen to others and possibly change my own mind, however unlikely. Name-calling and othering will never lead to mutual understanding or a change of heart. Hatred and revenge are common. Loving your enemy is for badasses.

After the wave from Bono, I joined Craig inside the coliseum lobby. We shuffled forward when the doors opened, and a scan of our tickets granted us admission into the Ellipse, the area in front of the stage inside the oval catwalk. Giddy with glee, we ran stage left to secure a spot in front of Adam Clayton, U2's bass player. Unbelievably (Craig will back me on this), Adam Clayton grinned at me for the entire show. Maybe he could sense my sheer elation. The same spiritual ecstasy filled me that I had felt as a teenager at church retreats. My spirit soared, my heart was at peace, and my mind was as clear as a mountain stream. The band finished with *40*, a suitable closing hymn for a transcendental experience. I left the show floating on air, joining the rest of the crowd in singing an acapella rendition of the lyrics U2 had lifted from the book of Psalms.

After the Charlotte show, Susan and I were eager to see the band again. For reasons now unclear to me, that show was in Mexico. Using our frequent flier miles to get to Monterrey on separate airlines, we booked a package. A crowd of 42,000 had been gathering for days at the Estadio Tecnológico for the opening of the fourth leg of the Vertigo Tour but we didn't want to spend the weekend standing in line. Anyway, our package included a free drink at a bar hosting a U2 tribute band. I found fake Bono disturbing, a knock-off doppelganger not lacking in talent for mimicry. We chugged our drink and headed to the venue for the Real Thing.

At the immense soccer stadium, Susan led us through the masses of people, her white hair parting the crowd like the staff of Moses. She spoke loudly in English, and we pretended not to understand Spanish as people complained about us cutting in line. My southern upbringing would never have allowed me to push through the crowd, but I wasn't ashamed enough to make her stop. Susan led us to a point where we couldn't get any closer; the crowd pressed in tight. In Mexico, personal space is not a thing. The concertgoers packed in so tightly no one could sit down for all the hours before the show. Although I had two days of antibiotics in me, I was exhausted by the time the show began. Strep had worn me down even though I was no longer contagious. When the band appeared on stage and the first chords of *Vertigo* filled the air, the man behind me began playing with my hair and singing in my ear in Spanish-accented English. Being a good Southern girl, I felt it would be rude to ask a strange man to stop touching my hair and singing in my ear.

And he didn't stop. For the entire show. It seemed an expression of camaraderie, a harmless if awkward, cultural difference. I sang the words to every song at the top of my voice despite the sore throat and a stranger's hands in my hair.

Early on Monday morning following the show, Susan and I headed to the airport for our separate flights home. Dressed in jeans and a concert T and carrying a cardboard tour poster, I stumbled onto my flight to Atlanta. At the ATL, I waited zombie-like for my connection back to North Carolina. I settled into my window seat after storing my poster in the overhead bin and opened the book I was reading about U2's Zoo TV tour in the '90s. I was startled when the person directly across the aisle leaned over and spoke.

"Hello, Suzanne. Are you returning from a conference?"

My eyes popped wide open as adrenaline shot through me. What are the freaking odds? I was surprised she even knew my name. She had only been president of the college for about a year. I could feel my face redden as a heat wave passed through my body. Wasn't I too old to get caught skipping school? Since I'm a terrible liar, I confessed the truth.

"No, I went to a U2 concert in Mexico."

I wouldn't get fired (I had informed my supervisor and filled out the requisite paperwork) but being on the bad side of the new president was not good. I prepared myself for a reproving glare and years of retribution.

"Oh," she replied cheerfully. "We met U2 years ago when I was in Russia working on a community health project. They were in the elevator with us at our hotel."

Thus began my great admiration of my college president. A seasoned traveler and a huge proponent of international education, she seemed to approve of a faculty member bold enough to attend a rock concert in another country by herself. As a "Yankee" and a woman, she had her work cut out for her in

Good Ol' Boy country. Over the next fifteen years, her progressive mindset put our college in the national spotlight for excellence. She would come to be my staunchest proponent, allowing me to experience many of my greatest adventures. In another four years, she would offer me the position of Director of International Education, a job that would take me literally around the world. Her support enabled me to create amazing programs with international and domestic students that would impact the lives of so many of them forever. She was the rare person in a position of power who earned my respect and admiration. And not only because she met U2.

*   *   *

My next U2 adventure was already penciled in before the Mexico concert: an eleven-day study abroad program to Ireland and the British Isles. I recruited a group of thirty-five people, enough to bring Craig and the kids along for free. These were the early days of study abroad when no rules had been established. I missed my kids when I led the groups in Costa Rica and Spain. I felt guilty about leaving them, worried I would screw up their psyches forever, even though Craig did a wonderful job of parenting, and the kids seemed perfectly fine. I assumed a lot of people thought I was a terrible mother for leaving my children for ten days every other year. I know my own mother did.

I wasn't a kid person growing up. I babysat on occasion as a teenager, but it was stressful. I still hadn't decided if I wanted kids when I got pregnant with Daniel. Up until the moment of his birth, I was worried if I'd like him. Fortunately, when he was born, the universe shifted, a shaft of sunlight shone on his face, and I was filled with a choking love unlike anything else I'd experienced. I still wasn't crazy about other people's kids, but my own were fabulous creatures – the most beautiful, hilarious, and smartest children ever born. But love comes at a great cost. As all parents know, that indescribable love comes with a range of fears – from their physical safety to their emotional well-being to their moral character. I understood the desire to protect them at all cost, but also knew that overprotection was a mistake. As every alchemist knows, to gain something of great value, something of equal value must be lost. Love makes you vulnerable.

I never dreamed I would be a take-your-children-to-Europe parent. My childhood vacations alternated between road trips to New Jersey to see my father's family and staying in a motel for a few days at Myrtle Beach. My dad served a year in Iceland in the Air Force when I was a baby, but other than that, my parents never left the United States. Though I felt guilty about traveling without my kids, I also felt guilty about taking them with me. I didn't want them to grow up with a rich kid mentality. However, I understood the power of travel to change people and wanted them to have a global perspective from an early age. It was worth the risk.

On their first transatlantic adventure, Anna was eight and her sole interest lay in any stray animal that crossed her path. Daniel, my prayed-for-nerd, was mildly interested in the educational aspects and looked forward to celebrating his twelfth birthday in London on the last day of the tour. They were both excited about our free afternoon family outing: stalking Bono. Daniel's favorite U2 song at the time was *Mysterious Ways*, in keeping with his theological and philosophical inclinations. Anna's pick was *Sunday, Bloody Sunday*, befitting her feistiness, though she didn't have all the lyrics right. Instead of *"Tonight, we can be as one,"* she sang *"Tonight, we can feed a swan."* Always the animal lover.

Flying into Shannon, patches of land in various shades of green materialized through the clouds as we landed. The Emerald Isle indeed. We gathered our bags and met our guide:

a middle-aged, British man named Mansel. Mansel could have been cast on Downton Abbey as a butler or valet, all priggish formality, restrained sighs, and a desert-dry wit. Our opinion of him changed when he performed a Monty Pythonesque reenactment of *Nicholas Nickleby* in a meeting room in our Dublin hotel that had us belly-laughing and shedding tears of uncontrolled mirth. Our bus driver was Phil from Cork, with a brogue so thick none of us could understand a word he said. Craig smoked his pipe with Phil at pit stops and chatted companionably. This impressed me until Craig confessed that he didn't understand Phil, either. I wasn't shocked that it doesn't matter to men if they don't understand a single word the other person is saying.

The first few days on the west coast of Ireland were a blur of fog, jet lag, and smoldering peat as we toured castles, cruised coastlines, and visited a bog village. On the Ring of Kerry, it rained so hard that nothing was visible through the fogged bus windows. At Blarney Castle. Anna and I climbed to the top of the crumbling ruin, but Daniel's fear of heights got the best of him, and Craig stayed on the ground with him. At age eight Anna was afraid to lie backward across the grated opening so many meters above the ground to kiss the smooth rock, so I was the only LaVenture to kiss the Blarney Stone. Craig says I already had the gift of gab, but I believe the cold kiss activated the smidge of my dormant Irish DNA and prepared me for all the conference presentations looming in my near future, unbeknownst to me.

We pulled into Dublin in the early evening with me peering out the bus window in case I caught a glimpse of The Edge strolling down the sidewalk. Bono wasn't in town, which pretty much ruined my plan. He was taking a ten-day trip to Africa. I love him for his work on behalf of the poorest of the poor, but I had been researching how to stalk him for eighteen months.

His decision to go to Africa ruined my plan to meet him fortuitously. Frankly, it was inconsiderate. Couldn't he have picked a different week to save the world? While he was off in Lesotho chatting with garment workers in textile factories, I had to settle for trying to run into Edge, Larry, or Adam. However, there's a part of me that doesn't want to meet Bono. I worry I'll say something stupid that will haunt me until the end of days. One of my life mottoes is *Fortune favors the bold*, but when it comes to meeting Bono, I think, *Better safe than sorry.*

On our Dublin city tour, I checked my watch constantly as we toured St. Patrick's Cathedral, Phoenix Park, and Temple Bar. Finally, the hands reached noon, time for our free afternoon in Dublin. I bid adieu to my students and headed off with my husband, children, Susan, and brilliant homeschooled Nick, who was also a U2 fan. As we scurried to the DART station, we passed Trinity College. A crowd queued to see the Book of Kells, an illuminated copy of the Gospels created by monks in the eighth century. I had more important things to see, namely, Bono's House. We took the train south, disembarked at Killiney station, and climbed a steep hill until we arrived at a square, white house. The front gate was framed by stone but covered with copper sheets engraved with U2 lyrics, lines from Yeats, sketches, and Scripture, as elaborately illuminated as the Book of Kells. The words EVERYTHING YOU KNOW IS WRONG stood out at the top, a possibility we should all contemplate regularly. We snapped photos, then picked wildflowers and stuck them between the bars on the gate.

We headed down an alleyway on the right side of the house. I picked up trash as we went, appalled that U2 fans would be litterbugs. We exited the passage onto the beach behind Bono's house and stared into the Irish Sea. Smooth, black stones dotted the sand, and I began to gather them, filling my purse and pockets. The shiny obsidian objects called to me as if they were talismans, imbued with powers of protection and rejuvenation. Weighed down by rocks, we headed back into Dublin to find out if my students had survived the afternoon. They were fine but spent most of their free time taking risqué photos with statues of renowned playwright Oscar Wilde and Molly Malone, famous fishmonger of song. I learned to play *Molly Malone* on the small electric organ I received for Christmas on my seventh birthday, an odd foreshadowing of my love affair with Ireland. During our dinner in Temple Bar, a trad band played other well-known tunes, the music as pure Irish as whiskey. Steve, one of our faculty members, joined in on the tin whistle, a bucket list item for him. You can barely take a step in Ireland without hearing music.

The next morning, a ferry chugged us across the Irish Sea to Wales, the Land of Song. Though U2's second most famous member, guitarist The Edge, was raised in Ireland, he was born in England to Welsh parents. Known for male voice choirs with harmonies and part singing, Welsh music is not only an art, but also a form of communication. In 1999, before the Wales-England Rugby match at Wembley Stadium, a chorus of men in red suit jackets and black bowties sang the famous Welsh hymn "Bread of Heaven," accompanied by none other than Sir Tom "Tiger" Jones. Wales defeated England by a single point in a match that is still remembered and celebrated today by the Welsh. My Aunt Nancy from New Jersey had been a huge Tom Jones fan when I was a kid and had traveled to Vegas often to see him. Maybe I get my singer-stalking from her.

We disembarked in Holyhead, boarded a bus with a new driver, and headed for Beaumaris, "the greatest castle never built." In the thirteenth century, Edward the first ordered the castle to be built but it was never completed, due to the cost of wars with Scotland. We had a bathroom stop in Llanfairpwllgwyngyllgogerychwyrndrobwllllantysiliogogogoch.

No, my cat didn't walk across my keyboard. This village took on the fifty-two-letter name in the late 1800s as a publicity gimmick to claim the longest place name in Europe. The Welsh word roughly translates to "The Church of Mary in the Hollow of the White Hazel near the Fierce Whirlpool and the Church of Tysilio by the Red Cave." Mansel pronounced it a couple of times and Daniel committed it to memory. He can pronounce it correctly to this day.

From Wales, we drove through the English Lakes District, then north to Scotland. We arrived at our Edinburgh hotel at dusk and dined on poorly cooked fish and chips and mushy peas. Steve's wife Sue complained about pain in her hip as she got off the bus. When the pain was still severe the next day, Mansel took her and Steve to the hospital while I stayed with the group for our city tour of Edinburgh Castle and Holyrood Palace. A kilted and white-bearded city guide named Robby amused us with his Scottish burr, trilling the letter R delightfully, but alarming us with vaguely sexist and racist comments. My kids ran around the castle as a bagpipe player busked at the entrance, and I was pleased for them to be at a real castle instead of a Disney castle. Haters can hate, but I'm not a Disney person. Though my daughter visited twenty countries as a child, she complained that she had never been to Disney World. Poor thing. (I did take her to Disney*land*, btw.) This is a minority opinion, but I don't understand paying outrageous sums of cash to stand in line under the sweltering sun for hours to see characters in costumes at a fake place. Give me the real places. Give me real people. Manufactured plastic happiness does not fill me up.

On the night we took the train from Edinburgh to London, we learned that Sue had fractured her hip. We had no choice but to leave her behind in Scotland with her husband Steve. Following surgery and a week-long stay in hospital, they were allowed to fly home. Her hospital bill upon release was zero.

Or to put it another way, there was no hospital bill. When she arrived back in the States, local physicians assured her she had received top-notch treatment and technically perfect surgery. My mother's claims that socialized medicine comes with long wait times and shoddy care were roundly disproven. Firsthand observation is the best way to find out the truth. A lifelong proponent of universal healthcare, my opinion has been reinforced by direct experience on multiple occasions.

The clock struck midnight as we boarded the train and found our assigned sleeping cars. Anna and I crammed ourselves into the tiny carriage with narrow bunk beds and a miniature sink while Craig and Daniel settled into an adjacent car. Like a cat, I find small spaces cozy and protective. As a side sleeper, my butt didn't hang over the bed ledge despite the narrowness. We chatted about our fun day in Scotland and what we wanted to see in London. The motion of the train lulled us to sleep, but the journey only took six hours, so we didn't get a full night's rest. Disembarking in England's ancient capital, we took off on a walking tour: from Buckingham Palace to Piccadilly Circus to St. Paul's Cathedral. Everything seemed new to me despite having spent my flu-plagued honeymoon in the city. The kids recognized Big Ben and the Tower Bridge, while Craig kept eyeing the pubs.

That evening we attended a multi-course medieval banquet, a four-course dinner and a show in a torchlit cellar near the Tower of London. Harps, lutes, and lyres provided a soothing ambiance as we were seated at a long wooden table. Knights, jesters, acrobats, and bards provided entertainment. We were forbidden from clapping but encouraged to bang our hands on the table. Daniel was super crabby until our serving wench selected him as the Lord of our group, after which he was quite content with the entire affair. He was especially fond of the cape he was given to wear. It was cheesy but our group got along well, and unlimited wine and beer flowed so it was a jovial evening.

Our last day in London, Daniel's twelfth birthday, was a free day. We wandered around the city trying to find affordable things to do that didn't cost a fortune. The exchange rate was terrible, so everything was super expensive. At the London aquarium, we viewed live sea creatures, and the kids made jellyfish out of paper plates, streamers, and plastic googly eyes. We strolled through Covent Garden and had lunch at a buffet in Chinatown. We snapped photos at Trafalgar Square and made the kids spend time in the National Gallery so they would develop an appreciation for art. (Okay, actually because it was free. Many museums are in London.) We joined the rest of the group at Piccadilly Circus for our farewell dinner at a famous fish 'n' chips shop. My students chortled at a poster on the wall advertising one of the restaurant's specials: Spotted Dick, a traditional British pudding. Mansel kindly arranged for a chocolate cake to be delivered to Daniel, so we could have a dickless dessert for his birthday. The wee Lord was pleased again.

Rising in the middle of the night, we boarded the bus for Heathrow. We bid farewell to Mansel, for whom we'd developed great affection. When we got to the airline counter, I hoisted my suitcase onto the scale. My luggage was overweight. This was embarrassing due to my repeated warnings to students not to overpack. I glanced around to see if any of them noticed.

"Whatcha have in your suitcase?" joked the airline employee. "Rocks?"

"Oh, yeah," I replied. She watched bemusedly as I unzipped my bag and shifted some of my rocks to my carry-on. "Bono rocks," I explained.

She started to respond, but shook her head, handed us our boarding passes, and pointed us toward security. I didn't know it was illegal to take rocks from an Irish beach, but my confession didn't faze her. I'm a fairly accomplished smuggler: rocks from Ireland, Cuban cigars from Costa Rica, *jamon ibérico* from Spain.

My kids passed through the airport like seasoned pros. The students brimmed with newfound confidence and strengthened friendships; the intergenerational mix of participants had resulted in unique connections and understanding. Sue was doing well in the Edinburgh hospital and Steve was happy with a few extra days in Scotland. Natalie, who had almost backed out at the last moment, had a life-altering experience and would go on to lead students abroad when she became a teacher. Danny had proposed to Tiffany over the bus mic in Wales, and they're married today with two fine boys. My son Daniel would eventually spend a semester at Oxford during undergrad. I would continue to try and meet Bono. Eleven days in the British Isles and Ireland had left permanent marks on many of us.

My Bono rocks now live in a ceramic bowl in my kitchen. I often carry one in my pocket and rub its smooth black surface while humming a U2 tune. My personal philosopher's stones provide peace of mind if not immortality. Carl Jung suggested that music is a psychic necessity, part of the collective unconsciousness. The mathematical precision of music blends with the mysterious elevation of the spirit, pure alchemical magic. Music bridges our conscious minds with our subconsciousness, a valuable tool to bring light to our path. Whenever I'm stuck in a moment, blasting U2 and singing at the top of my lungs lifts me up and illuminates my way. Participating in the universal act of song reminds me of the things that bind us all together.

THE DOMINICAN REPUBLIC:
WOMAN PLANS, GOD LAUGHS

The raucous conga line threaded through the white plastic chairs in the dusty church courtyard. Above the sound of the music blasting from the loudspeakers, above the beat of the drums and the rhythm of the accordion, I could hear God chuckling at me. The whole town turned out for the special service, the women in mismatched skirts and T-shirts and the children in ill-fitting clothes that had been donated by people in the States, ironically adorned with the logos and catchphrases of consumerism. Dominicans and Americans placed their hands on the waists of the person in front of them and shuffle-kicked around the unpaved patio moving chairs out of the way as needed. The Spirit was moving and so were we. No snoring in the pews at this service. Despite all the noise, God's laughter rang in my ears. He loves a good joke at my expense.

A group of eye doctors were putting on a weeklong clinic in the Dominican Republic and I had volunteered as an interpreter. However, instead of helping with vision patients, I was assigned to interpret at a loose version of Vacation Bible School. Each day a hundred kids from toddler to teen gathered on the covered cement slab to sing and do crafts and watch dramatic reenactments of Bible stories. It was a far cry from the cool, age-segregated church basement of my childhood. Excitement buzzed as the kids ran and skipped to the pavilion every morning. Many didn't attend school regularly and none of them had phone or computer screens at home. They talked with their friends and roughhoused, but we managed to mostly keep their attention though we were hoarse from yelling over them at the end of the day. They had a good ability to focus, even the teenage boys were happy to color a picture for half an hour. The long muggy days of VBS on a cement slab were exhausting, but I delighted in acting out the role of Rebecca in Spanish, encouraging my son Jacob to trick his dad into giving him his brother Esau's birthright. You think God would have been satisfied with that, but no, He had something bigger in mind for me.

Reading and writing perfect Spanish was a breeze by the time I finished college, but speaking was a different matter. When speaking, there's no time to dissect each sentence and scrutinize grammar. For many years I spoke Spanish as little as possible in front of native Spanish speakers. My goodness, I might make an error. ¡*Imagínense*! (Plural formal imperative mood with reflexive pronoun attached, accent added to shift emphasis to the proper syllable.) Proud of myself for agreeing to accompany ophthalmologists to a tropical island, I envisioned helpfully asking patients ¿*Cuál es mejor? ¿Uno o dos?* as they peered into a machine. That seemed like a feasible task, but God had a far bigger stretch in mind.

My second-grade teacher is partially responsible for my perfectionism hang-up. She made us memorize this saying: "Good, better, best. Never, ever rest until your good is better and your better is your best." Evil witch. I should send her my therapy bills. I had transferred into her class in November because my family had moved, and she made me stand in the bathroom on my first day because I cried. Lesson learned: Crying is for losers. No more of that. She made us spell a word each day before going outside to recess, and once she discovered I could spell anything, she began giving me words like supercalifragilistic-expialidocious. I felt vindicated when I received the trophy for most books read at the end of the year even though I started at the school three months after the other kids. Another lesson learned: I could use my brain to stand out and collect awards and respect. However, even being the best wasn't enough; perfection was the goal.

I figured my Spanish would impress the people of the DR as long as no one knew I taught college Spanish, which in my mind meant I should never make a mistake. My master's degree in Spanish literature implied that I have *mastered* the Spanish language. I was okay with a few minor mistakes in one-on-one conversations (even though I might lose sleep upon remembering them in the middle of the night). I was dang proud of myself for offering to be an interpreter, considering that my one paid interpreter gig a decade prior had been a humiliating disaster. (Hired to interpret for a group of Spaniards touring a compressor factory, I had discovered that I know zero compressor-related words in English or Spanish. Oil-flooded rotary screw compressor? Male and female rotors? Extrusion blow molding? It had been a nightmare.) Interpreting in the DR was like getting back on the horse ten years after I fell off.

After the short flight to the D.R., our group clambered onto a private bus to take us from Puerto Plata to El Catey, a tiny town at the base of the lobster-claw-shaped Samaná peninsula. The doctors and church volunteers claimed seats on the bus, chatting about the plan for the week. As we barreled down the potholed "road," traffic zoomed around us from all directions. Mopeds with entire families perched precariously on top like circus acrobats weaved around animals and small children lounging by the roadside. As we zigzagged through the human obstacle course, I took deep breaths, sent up a prayer, and stopped looking out the window. I later read a list on the Internet that rates Dominican drivers as the seventh worst in the world. They deserve a higher ranking, in my opinion.

We arrived at the compound without running over anyone. The bus passed through a gate in a chain link fence and then passed the open shelter with a concrete slab floor and a pitched green roof where we would hold VBS. We parked at a white rectangular building flanked by swaying palm trees. Our hosts were a missionary doctor and his wife. They were an odd couple: a tall, athletic man and his small, quiet wife who prepared delicious meals for us. A weird tension ran between them, and I wasn't sure they liked each other. They lived on the top floor of the building, with the bottom floor reserved for the church teams who came regularly to build things, conduct VBS for the local kids, or run medical clinics. Stacks of bunk beds covered by mosquito netting lined the ground floor: ladies to the right, gents to the left. No AC, of course. The generator only provided electricity for a few hours a day. We were allowed a five-minute cold bucket shower in the small indoor bathroom, but all our business was to be conducted in the outhouse constructed by a previous church team. Made of brick and concrete, it had toilet tissue, and it was nice as far as outhouses go. It didn't smell great, but it was spacious.

And then there were the spiders. Not itsy-bitsy spiders charmingly climbing up a waterspout. Not sweet Charlotte spinning important messages in lovely webs. I'm talking Shelob-stab-you-in-the-dark-of-Mordor mother-effin' *spiders*. Snakes terrify me more than bugs, but I can't say I'm a fan of *giant* spiders. Other oversized insects hung out with the spiders on the cement patio outside our door, including scorpions. As we sat there in the evenings reflecting on our day, my eyes roamed from one dreadful creature to the next. A trip to the outhouse at night was unthinkable. I risked dehydration in the evenings to avoid death by heart attack in the dark. I had mentally prepared myself for the trip, ready to ally myself with the people of the DR and abandon all my worldliness, but on arrival, my inner

American princess was screaming. Sleeping on the top bunk in an unairconditioned insectarium with a dozen semi-strangers and no bathroom? I was more attached to my privilege than I thought.

After a day or so of getting to know people who lived in worse conditions for their entire lives, my inner diva piped down. The eye doctors put things in perspective. They alternated years between Haiti and the D.R. and described how Haiti was so much worse even though the two countries shared one island. In Haiti, the poorest nation in the western hemisphere, armed guards accompanied the doctors everywhere for their protection. Conditions are wretched and disease is rampant. The doctors wore masks in the shower to protect their orifices from being infested with parasitic worms from the water. I stopped listening after that.

The first night, Michael, the trip leader, asked me to go with him to visit a family he knew from earlier visits. I had decided to go on this trip because of Michael. He had been taking the Spanish class I was teaching on Wednesday nights at my church, and since he wasn't exactly fluent, he encouraged me to come to the DR as an interpreter with his church. Michael was a tall and large red-headed man with a gentle spirit. By day, he was an engineer, but his heart was for missions. He had been to the DR several times before and was beloved by many in the town.

As night began to fall, Michael, a college student named Tess, and I set off down the dirt road. We passed houses made from cinder blocks, wooden slats, and random pieces of tin roofing.

"*Buenas tardes*," women sitting outside greeted us and waved as we went by.

"*Buenas tardes*," we replied and waved as the sun sank.

As we walked Michael told us about the family we were visiting. He told us the names of the parents and their surviving children. "They lost their eighteen-month-old daughter last year. She fell into a hole in their yard and died."

"Oh my gosh. How awful." Tess and I exchanged looks of horror.

"Tragedies are common here," Michael added. "So many sad stories."

It was mind-boggling to think that a toddler could die in such a way and that it wasn't even out of the ordinary. How did people endure such cruel and tragic lives? How did they hold onto their faith?

Darkness fell by the time we arrived at a one-room shack held together with pieces of corrugated metal and sticks. The dwelling was longer than it was wide, barely accommodating a dilapidated sofa. The home wasn't fully enclosed; holes and gaps permeated the walls and floor. The parents greeted Michael, rising from the sofa with smiles on their faces to shake his hand and hug him despite his disproportionate size. Michael handed them a bag of used clothing for their other kids, and they thanked him many times. We sat in a row on a sofa-like lump and watched television, an apparatus that seemed futuristic in the shabby room. Viewing *Sábado Gigante* via satellite in a barely standing structure ranks as one of the most surreal experiences of my life. I watched the family, mesmerized by the jarring contrast of them laughing at the antics of Don Francisco while pain never left their faces. I had seen poverty on this level in Colombia, but it was from a distance. Meeting people with names and histories in their homes made it real. We were subdued as we made our way back to the compound.

Michael was quiet except to remind us to watch our step in the dark. His compassion was deep; his heart broke for these people. His gentleness and selflessness were qualities I didn't often see in men, and I confess to having a wee crush on him while we were in the D.R. I understand the irony of indulging in adulterous fantasies while on a mission trip. Still, I daydreamed our spouses would painlessly vanish so he and I could renounce all earthly goods and travel the globe Helping Others and Doing Good. While our living conditions would be tough, our hearts would be full of purpose and joy. The fantasy centered on filling that God-shaped hole, which I was constantly trying to fill with love, food, approval, travel.

While this do-gooder fantasy may not appeal to everyone, it is totally in keeping with my role as "the hero child" in my family of origin. My mother's strict rules and staunch faith molded me into a person you can count on to do the right thing. While my sister Cindy rebelled from our rigid upbringing at an early age, I mainly kept to the straight and narrow. Cindy was so "bad" that it didn't take much to look good. No one seemed to suspect that her outrageous behavior stemmed from trauma and emotional neglect. From our mother we learned our anger; from our father we learned humor. No one taught us to deal with feelings of pain or sadness or disappointment or doubt. Rage and laughter were our only two options.

Though Baptists stress salvation by grace and not by works, good works seemed to bring me closest to feeling whole. Since college, I've donated to charities and volunteered in soup kitchens and women's shelters. For a dozen years, I went to jail on Tuesday nights with other women from my church. The Spirit showed up at the detention center every week, a sense of hope and compassion traveling through our clasped hands as we prayed for court dates and children and peace of mind. I still give cash to people experiencing homelessness, and occasionally even a ride. My therapist gasps in horror at my "lack of boundaries," but as a non-believer, she doesn't totally get me. True faith is about radical selflessness. The less I focus on myself, the more content I am.

While I still believe that caring for others is the best way to feel less self-absorbed, doing the right thing also results in praise for selfless acts. Which makes them not so selfless. Altruism is another path to earning love and admiration. My husband often scolds me for taking on too much, but how can I let my reputation as the responsible, reliable, and compassionate one falter? The guilt and shame I feel for letting someone down is greater than the cost of just doing the thing. Much is required of she-to-whom-much-is-given. I've seen how fortunate I am compared to millions of others in this world. My week in the Dominican Republic humbled me, reminding me that my sacrifices are truly minimal and subtly driven by making myself feel good. God doesn't actually need my help.

The wrongness of my fantasies about Michael didn't bother me much since I had zero intention of acting on them. I'm pretty sure our politics clashed. And despite his gentleness, he might have been the type of man who expected his wife to cook or listen to him. Being the Good Girl prevents me from having a physical affair, but in light of what my Southern Baptist, tee-to-taling, Sunday School teacher father did, I wonder if there are circumstances that would have led me to cross that line. However, at this point, his actions were still unthinkable to all of us.

There were few married couples in the town of El Catey. Most of the men had left in search of work, leaving behind wives and girlfriends, most with multiple children. None of the kids had a lot, but some showed signs of severe nutritional deficiencies with dry, scaly skin and hair that was turning white. A twelve-year-old Dominican boy could easily be mistaken for an eight-year-old American boy. Sometimes we ventured out of the compound to buy a soda at the tiny store down the street. Kids would tag along in the hope of getting a treat, but how to buy something for one but not all? The children hung around the store not overtly asking for anything and facing glares from the shopkeeper. I bought something for whoever was there, despite the risk of being mobbed the next time I went to the store. I'm a believer in the starfish story. I can't help everyone, but I can make a real difference to a few.

One afternoon after another exhausting day of Vacation Bible School on the concrete slab, I left the compound with some others from our group and strolled the dusty streets. The warm sun shone on us as we greeted the people and meandered through the town. A gorgeous white sand beach and fancy vacation rentals were a mere mile away, but you never would have guessed it from the town. We passed block and cement homes, a corner store, a dilapidated school. I was stunned when several in our group seemed anxious and expressed the desire to get back to the compound. They were afraid. I couldn't believe it. A bubble of rage rose in my heart. What was there to be afraid of? Never mind that I had far more travel experience than most of them, spoke fluent Spanish, and have a high tolerance for risk. God likes to remind me of my hypocrisy and often seems to derive a fair amount of pleasure from it.

The next day He reminded me of my fear of not speaking perfect Spanish. On the infamous evening in question, when Michael asked me to interpret while he preached, I reluctantly agreed even though simultaneous interpretation has been proven to be as mentally stressful as brain surgery. I'm a good translator (written), but interpretation (oral) is a whole different thing. But it would seem surly to refuse since I had come along as an interpreter. Mission trips make it damn near impossible to get out of doing the right thing. I tamped down my anxiety by trying to convince myself that no one would attend a weeknight service. The small church had just a few meager pews. How bad could it be? We arrived at the church near dusk and to my horror townspeople were setting out dozens of rickety plastic chairs in the dusty courtyard. Giant loudspeakers and a microphone were wheeled in. A *microphone*. So, although Michael preached, it was me the entire town heard. This was my worst nightmare come to life. It didn't help that I could hear God cackling the whole time. "You're afraid to speak Spanish in front of native speakers? Here's an entire town of *hispanohablantes* listening to you simultaneously interpret for half an hour without a pause." As they say, God comforts the afflicted and afflicts the comfortable. He seems particularly delighted to push me out of my comfort zone. I can't entirely blame Him since I do the same thing to my students.

I had the foresight to ask Michael his topic and read the passage in my Spanish-language Bible before the service. Shockingly, in all my years of school, I had never learned how to say "sheaves of wheat" or "Nebuchadnezzar" in Spanish. In retrospect, this seems like an odd sermon for an outdoor broadcast in a tiny town on the northern coast of a poor Caribbean Island. However, I have a fondness for the Book of Daniel, not only the fiery furnace and the lion's den, but also the bizarro, apocalyptic dream sequences. I love Daniel's courage in speaking truth to power, though I cannot relate to his rebuffing the king's rich food and wine and insisting on eating vegetables and drinking water. Despite that unfathomable decision, I named my first-born son Daniel. If the Daniel of the Bible could face lions and fiery furnaces, surely I could endure a spotlight, a microphone, and a crowd of friendly faces.

I got through the sermon, my voice booming over the giant speakers for all to hear. My Spanish wasn't perfect, but it was good enough. (Such a difficult concept for me.) I interpreted the final prayer and said *"Amén."* Music blasted from the loudspeaker. Instead of dispersing, the crowd began clapping their hands and singing. The song turned into dancing and a conga line formed around the rows of plastic chairs. The adrenaline in my body subsided as I watched the jubilant worshipers parade around the courtyard. After some urging, I joined the line of joyful dancers and worshiped God. In fact, I threw back my head and laughed right along with Him.

I'm pretty sure that's what He was going for all along.

ACROSS EUROPE: HORRORS
BIG AND SMALL

The first shocking thing about Auschwitz was the beauty of it. The bus curved west through the lush Polish countryside from Krakow. The sun shone and a warm breeze stirred the trees. Clouds gathered as we neared the camp, but rays of sunlight broke through, illuminating the green grass and neat brick buildings. We passed through the iconic gate under the infamous sign: *Arbeit macht frei.* Work sets you free. A cruel joke? A false promise? A warped truism? Deceptive sunlight and a gentle breeze accompanied us into the death camp.

According to a recent article in the Washington Post, two-thirds of American millennials cannot identify Auschwitz. My students and I shivered silently in front of glassed-in rooms displaying mangled eyeglasses and prostheses, piles of mismatched shoes, a mountain of human hair degraded by time. A single suitcase with a name and address carefully printed in block letters can break you. The grim gaze of one child's face below roughly shorn hair twists your guts. She could be yours. What happened to this girl was an abomination. How could it have been repeated millions of times? Some people deny it happened at all. My students know better. They've seen it with their own eyes. They will never forget the piles of individual property, the crumbling crematoria, the firing squad wall. You can read books and watch movies about the holocaust, but ghosts pass through you as you walk through Auschwitz.

★ ★ ★

Our Central Europe program was a whirlwind—five countries in ten days (Hungary, Czech Republic, Poland, Slovakia, Germany). The group of students and community members was great, and everyone was eager to absorb all the history, no matter how painful. However, the Central Europe tour almost never happened because the tour I led to Spain, France, and Italy two years earlier was so horrible. That disastrous experience almost ended my international education career before it really started. People who have never led groups abroad often assume the job is a free vacation. Just close your eyes and imagine for a minute how much work it takes to plan, market, recruit, prepare, and manage a bunch of community college students in another country. From salesperson to bill collector to bad cop to understanding parent, you've got to wear a lot of hats. It's an incredible amount of work, especially if you do it right. It takes a special kind of crazy to take students abroad—not only a crazy love of travel but also a crazy belief in the power of travel to transform people's lives.

The Spain-France-Italy group seemed determined to prove that they were immune to being changed by seeing the world. Toward the end of the program, one of the families, a mom (the student), a dad, and their teenage son could be heard shouting from the floor above about how their room in Rome sucked. I felt mystified; we were lodged in a fine hotel with a gorgeous rooftop view of the Eternal City. Granted, in true European style there was only one small elevator, and it took a while for thirty-three people and thirty-three suitcases to get to their rooms. The showers were also typically European: a tile floor with a drain and a wall-mounted, removable shower head. This apparently pushed them over the edge. A rude and ill-tempered redhead traveling with her grandmother also pitched a fit about the rooms; I heard rumors that they and the other family were threatening to take taxis to a different hotel. Good riddance. I had spoken with all of them repeatedly about their attitudes and tried to encourage them to make the most of the experience. It was thanks to these participants that I developed my five rules of study abroad which I've shared with every subsequent group:

5. No whining (This is only two weeks of your life.)

4. No whining (Not everyone gets the opportunity to travel.)

3. No whining (You can do hard things.)

2. No whining (Different is not the same as bad.)

1. No whining (People will form opinions about Americans based on your behavior.)

In addition to the crappy attitudes and constant complaints, one girl with rainbow tattoos vomited repeatedly on the bus, claiming motion sickness. I suspected it was due to massive hangovers and/or continuous drunkenness. Though this young woman was nineteen, she had back trouble and could barely walk. In the pre-departure meetings, I stressed that we would be doing fast-paced walking tours of every city. Even the "good" students had issues. A polite lovely young woman had chronic gastric issues, including an emergency at the Palais des Papes in Avignon. The whole group yawned with boredom as we toured the Papal seat of fourteenth century Christianity in the South of France. At dinner that night, they complained about the fish we were served and headed off to the McDonald's down the road. They reported back that no one spoke English there. I wanted to bang my head against the wall. Luckily, Craig was with me and I could vent my frustrations, though I tried to do it out of earshot of our kids.

In Barcelona, a blonde, curly-haired student had to pee every fifteen minutes. She said this was normal for her, that she always peed every fifteen minutes. This did not seem normal to me, especially when she said she slept through the night. We spent our free afternoon with her strolling *Las Ramblas*, the famous tree-lined pedestrian street. Craig, Anna, and I laughed as a street performer dressed as Edward Scissorhands pretended to cut Daniel's hair, while this student darted in and out of every restaurant in search of a bathroom.

Then there was Ian. Ian had traveled on the British Isles tour two years before but now was determined to drink his way through Europe. When he drunkenly arrived thirty minutes after the appointed time with a huge grin on his face, Craig had to hold me back from throttling him. Finally, there was another mother-daughter combo in which the mother was a delightful human being but had somehow raised a horrible child. The daughter was in her mid-thirties with the attitude of a petulant teenager. Our tour director, Alberto, was a laid-back Spaniard who didn't seem to care that our group possessed an abundance of *idiotas*. I half appreciated his lack of judgment, but half wished for a stern Mansel-type who would jerk a knot into my students.

I was tired and cranky when we rolled into Florence. Ian's sister, who was not on my bad list, had been complaining about a boil on her inner thigh. I told her to put a Band-Aid on it and keep walking. At eleven o'clock at night she knocked on my door, insisting she needed to see a doctor. Begrudgingly, I resigned myself to taking her to the emergency room, which was within walking distance of the hotel. I threw on some clothes along with the scowl on my face. As we made our way through the streets of *Firenze*, the miracle happened. The church bells from Giotto's tower at the Duomo began ringing, and Brunelleschi's magnificent dome illuminated the night sky. People began to line the ancient stone-paved street. A procession of priests and nuns in robes and garments of assorted colors and designs filed by. They sang as they processed, some holding hymnals, some with candles or other religious objects. As a Protestant, I have no words for the garments they wore or the items they carried, but it was holy. I felt like Samwise Gamgee seeing the passing of the elves shortly after leaving the Shire. We watched in silent awe until the sacred parade passed. I never would have witnessed the mystical procession had I not been taking a student to the ER late at night.

The hospital itself was surreal in a different way: more like a Stephen King novel. We wandered empty corridors but finally found the entrance to the Emergency Department. The facility was deserted and creepy, but we didn't have to wait long. An English-speaking physician treated the boil (which I admit merited attention by a doctor.) We left with a prescription for a special cream to take to a local pharmacy the next day. Of course, there was no bill. Damned socialized medicine again. Taking care of people quickly and efficiently all for free. What a crazy concept.

Witnessing the mystical procession of the clergy made me briefly more tolerant of my students for the next couple of days, but things came to a head when we arrived in Rome. The students pitched a fit about their rooms, but I hoped a full day in the city would calm them the eff down. The morning grew hot as a local city guide schlepped us around to the Colosseum, Forum, and Vatican. Outside the Sistine Chapel, our guide pointed at a small replica of the ceiling and spent twenty-five minutes describing what we would see when allowed to enter. Most of the group couldn't hear her and the ones who could were bored. For once, I couldn't blame them. Finally, the doors to the Chapel opened and I stood under Michelangelo's master-piece with a group of rural community college students. All of us craned our necks to take in the ceiling, God's finger reaching out to create Adam. I had another moment of peace, satisfied that I had a hand in bringing these people to this incredible place. The Last Judgment, which covers the entire altar wall, is equally impressive. Look closely at the details of men being pulled down by demons and it will literally scare the hell out of you. Little did I know, I was about to let loose on my group in a miniature version of Judgment Day.

The guards shooed us out of the Chapel, and into St. Peter's Square. Alberto nonchalantly mentioned that since it was Sunday we could stick around for the Papal Blessing if we were interested. Even though the Pope at the time was Benedict, I was not going to pass up the opportunity to see the Pontiff IRL. We stood in the hot sun with masses of people from all over the world. Promptly at noon, the Bishop of Rome appeared at the window of his apartment and greeted the crowd in so many languages I lost count. The Holy Father continued his remarks in Italian, and I caught most of it. With my zillion years of Spanish and two semesters of Italian, I speak a mean *Spitalian* (65 percent Spanish; 35 percent Italian.) After concluding with the *Angelus*, Benedict slipped back into his apartment and the crowd dispersed.

Alberto insisted we eat lunch at a super expensive cafeteria off St. Peter's Square. Cranky from standing in the sun and paying a fortune for a mediocre lunch, our group resumed our forced march, off to see the rest of Rome. Castel Sant Angelo. Pantheon. Trevi Fountain. I admit it wasn't the most fun day I've ever had, but we were in the ancient capital of stoicism, my favorite philosophy. Virtue is sufficient for happiness; self-control should keep negative emotions in check; patient endurance of unpleasant situations is wise and necessary. However, most of the group were not familiar with the teachings of Seneca, Marcus Aurelius, or Epictetus.

We paused at the top of one of Rome's seven hills and I did a quick count, something I do constantly with students abroad. Thirty-one, damn! Who are we missing? A quick scan revealed that the missing persons were the rainbow-tattoo-bus-vomiter and the grown woman with the adolescent attitude.

"Where are Renée and Katie?" I demanded.

After a few sheepish glances, a small voice spoke. "They're not coming."

"They're not coming? What do you mean they're not coming?" I screeched. How could they not be coming? We were a group of thirty-three people in the middle of Rome. Our hotel was miles away on the outskirts of the city. They had to be coming.

"They said it's too hot and they're tired and they're not walking up the hill."

This was the proverbial last straw.

"Go get them," I growled. "I am old, and I am fat, and if I can walk up this hill, so can they."

When the two defectors finally schlepped up the hill, thunderous looks on their faces, I let the whole group have it. My frustrations about their behavior over the past ten days poured out. My stoic demeanor failed me. In other words, I lost my shit. I told them I was ashamed of how they had represented our college and our country. They were the kind of people who give Americans a bad name in the world. They didn't appreciate the amazing opportunity they'd been given. I was sorry I had brought them. When I finally finished my rant, they appeared chastened. Several of the well-behaved kids muttered, "About time." It was the first and only time I yelled at an entire group. I was convinced in that moment that there was no way I'd ever take students abroad again. My passion for sharing a global perspective with young minds dissipated in the hot Italian afternoon.

In retrospect, I'm not sorry I took them. At least half of the people in the group were wonderful and I believe even the difficult ones did not remain unchanged by the experience. Over the years, the study abroad committee worked hard to improve the way we prepare students to travel abroad. Research shows you don't gain cultural competence merely through travel, but through preparation and reflection on the experience. It's difficult for students who have lived an insulated, rural life to be thrust into a literal whole new world. I had been baptized by fire in Bogotá, but I possessed an inner resilience not all my students have. Now each student is required to write a daily journal addressing reflective prompts. The required class not only covers travel basics but also explains cultural difference and provides country-specific information. One twelve-day tour of Europe is not going to remake a person, but with good pre-departure instruction and critical reflection, it can be a transformative experience.

At the time, though, I vowed I would never lead another group. The following fall I switched from teaching on the main campus to a tiny satellite campus. The student body consisted mainly of Early College students who earn an associate's degree while simultaneously completing their high school diploma. At first, I was afraid I wouldn't like teaching high schoolers, but I soon developed affection for the kids and the no-drama atmosphere of the campus. I did my job, and I went home. No International Club, no International Night, no office next to a colleague who did half the work I did for the same pay. This blissful arrangement of teaching and nothing more lasted for eighteen months.

One fateful afternoon, I was summoned to the small conference room. Knees trembling slightly, I greeted the president and the vice president of the college. Both were blonde, impeccably dressed, and smiling. I glanced at my wrinkled pants and wished I had gone over them with Scotch tape to remove some of the cat hair.

"Hello, Suzanne," the VP oozed. "We want to talk to you about taking on the role of Director of International Education."

My heart thudded and I risked a glance at the President who nodded and smiled.

"We'll be able to offer you a one course teaching reduction in addition to a small stipend."

Ka-thump, ka-thump, ka thump. This was a fool's bargain. Take on a second full-time job in exchange for a 17 percent reduction in my current workload? Build an international program across two campuses while still teaching fifteen credit hours each semester from the smaller campus? It was a fool's bargain.

"I'd love to. Thanks so much for this opportunity," I gushed.

My insides were tumbling but a smile spread across my face. I loved teaching and I was good at it. I was the only faculty member who had won the College's teaching award in two separate years. I was a semi-finalist for the State Teaching Award in 2001, but my interview fell on 9/11, and I didn't go because it seemed a weird time to talk about my accomplishments and Craig didn't want me driving to Raleigh anyway. However, I had learned that whatever students learned in my classroom paled compared to what they could learn in a brief time in another country. I was passionate about international education and committed to bringing opportunities for global learning to rural community college students. Plus, I was still carrying an almost full class load, so I wouldn't have to give up teaching anyway.

The first study abroad program I led with my new title was to Central Europe in 2010. There were a lot of Early College students on the tour, and I learned that seventeen-year-old high school students are much easier than eighteen-year-old college students who think they're adults. From soaking in the thermal baths in Budapest, to placing our hands on the remnants of the Berlin wall, to standing under the astronomical clock in Prague, to our sacred, haunting visit to Auschwitz, this program reinvigorated my passion for taking students abroad.

The only glitch was in Prague, when Caleb, an Early College student, got separated from his friends in the Old Town Square and couldn't find his way back to the hotel. Students woke me at midnight to tell me he hadn't come back. I was panicked and my first thought was to run around the city looking for him. Our guide Jurgen assured me that wasn't practical, so I sat outside the hotel asking every taxi driver who arrived: "Have you seen a Black kid?" Since he was pretty much the only person of color in the city, I figured there was a chance.

Finally, one of the cabs pulled up and Caleb got out. Filled with relief, I bellowed: "Where were you?" as I gave him a hug. Not only was Caleb one of my favorite students, but his dad was a cop. I had spent most of my time waiting imagining what I would say on a phone call to his parents. Thank God I didn't have to make that call. Caleb had known we were at an Ibis hotel but hadn't realized that was the name of the chain and not an individual hotel. He'd taken the subway until it closed, then walked for miles. At the fourth Ibis he tried, he finally found the right hotel. I can't say I've never lost a study abroad participant, but mercifully it was a temporary loss with a happy conclusion. I didn't even yell at him when days later he ran through the halls of our Soviet-style hotel in Krakow in his newly purchased Speedo.

As it turned out, this was the last trip of its kind for me. Once I became the Director of International Education, things changed quickly. I was soon working sixty to seventy hours per week, but that's okay because I'm a Boomer and my kids were teenagers. The hours I dedicated to my career reflect my generation's work ethic, my need for achievement, and my belief that what I do makes a difference in other people's lives. I can't abide the thought of being ordinary. When the program was handed to me, it consisted of a troika partnership to take four students to China each year with two other colleges. We were also hosting three international students from Egypt through a State Department program to bring non-elite students to community colleges. Little did anyone know that it was just the beginning. I didn't exactly plan on building a nationally-recognized program, but that's where we were headed.

MACEDONIA: MY BIG FAT
MACEDONIAN EASTER

I stare down at the endangered trout on my plate. Irina and Nikola smile proudly.

"We make special arrangements for you to try."

"Thank you," I smile queasily, thinking about the previous week when conservationist Jeff Corwin was on campus talking about the preservation of imperiled species. Five thousand miles from home, I glance around the restaurant table at the faces of the most hospitable people I've ever met. Irina and Nikola have gone to great lengths to procure the speckled Ohrid trout for our Holy Saturday dinner despite the fishing ban preventing its consumption. Lake Ohrid is one of Europe's oldest and deepest lakes, straddling the border between North Macedonia and Albania. The trout is only protected on the Macedonian side of the lake; the fish in Albanian waters are fair game. If they were smart, the trout would stay on the Macedonian side, but fish aren't known for their intellect. Since my dinner gave its life in my honor, I proclaim delight with every bite. It's good, but it doesn't taste that different from non-almost-extinct trout.

A little before midnight, Irina and Nikola announce it's time to go, so we leave everything as is on the table and wind our way through narrow streets, up a hill to an ancient Byzantine church. We celebrated Easter at home the Sunday before but are curious to experience Orthodox traditions. It is drizzling as we stand in the stone courtyard and a crowd holding candles gathers around us. At midnight, the priest pounds three times on the door of the church with a wooden hammer to symbolize Christ's victory over Hades. The church doors swing open, and we enter, the air filled with singing and incense. Our friends kiss the icons along the church walls and greet one another with cries of Христос Воскресе (Christ is risen), echoed by the reply of Вистина Воскресе (Indeed He is risen). There is no service, no sermon or choir, just a Christmas Eve feeling of candles in the dark and a proclamation of Good News.

We return to the restaurant and finish dinner with the famous Ohrid cake consisting of multiple layers of caramel, walnuts, and chocolate. We drink strong Macedonian coffee, not worrying about it interfering with our sleep. Our friends teach us the Easter egg cracking game. A bowl of hard-boiled eggs appears on the table, all dyed a deep red. Each person takes an egg and clinks it against another person's egg. If you crack your friend's egg and yours stays unbroken, you win the round. The last intact egg wins. As we crack away, a trio of accordion, bass and violin plays in the background. We toast my colleague Vinnie, the winner, with many glasses of *rakija*, potent Macedonian brandy. Dancing ensues.

Vinnie and I were in Macedonia to provide a week-long workshop to the Hospitality and Tourism faculty at the University of St. Kliment. Irina, a Professor of Linguistics at UKLO, had obtained a grant from the U.S. Embassy for a professional development seminar related to American culture. Vinnie was the head of the culinary program at a community college in Maryland, and I was the American culture expert. Irina served as a Fulbright Scholar-in-Residence at my college in the fall of 2010, my first full semester as Director of International Education. Craig and I got to know her and Nikola well during their semester in North Carolina. Now, to my surprise and delight, I was cracking eggs, drinking brandy, and dancing with my husband in the richly historic but politically new Republic of Macedonia.

I learned a lot about Macedonia during Irina's semester in North Carolina. Before that, I probably could have told you it was a place mentioned in the Bible and that I was pretty sure it used to be a part of Yugoslavia. Thousands of years before that, the ancient kingdom of Macedonia belonged to Greece and became the definitive Hellenistic state. Alexander the Great was born there in 356 BC and expanded the empire to Africa and India. The ancient Macedonian territory was much larger than the modern country, but Greece still claims the name. In fact, Greece was not at all happy about the country being called the Republic of Macedonia when they became a separate nation in 1991.[1] Since 1944, Macedonia had been a part of Tito's Yugoslavia. Political upheaval in the early 1990s led to the breakup of Yugoslavia into seven separate Balkan countries. So, while touring this twenty-year old country, we visited the Bay of Bones, a recreation of a prehistoric settlement estimated to be over 3000 years old. A good reminder that borders are not fixed boundaries; these imaginary lines change all the time.

In the wee hours of Easter Sunday, Nikola returned us to our charming hotel overlooking Lake Ohrid. The *rakija* overpowered the coffee and we slept like rocks. At noon on Sunday, Nikola picked us up again. His tiny car was redolent with an enticing aroma. Was I having anticipatory hallucinations on the way to Easter lunch? Something smelled delicious. At the Petrovski home, Craig and I disengaged ourselves from the small backseat. I stifled a scream as Nikola popped the trunk and revealed a small, cooked dinosaur in a large aluminum pan. Actually, it was a lamb, but I had never seen anything like it

---

1 In January of 2019, the name was changed to Republic of North Macedonia, which pacified the Greeks a bit.

– head and hooves attached and roasted, teeth bared and empty eye sockets staring. It gave me quite a start despite the yummy smell. By the time Irina carved the lamb and placed it on the platter, it looked like any plate of meat. It was delicious, but I will never forget the shock of seeing a cooked dinosaur in the trunk of a car.

Irina greeted us with many kisses as we entered their spacious home, a former Turkish school. Two tables had been pushed together in the living room to accommodate the friends, family, and an array of enticing dishes. Following a blessing, we stuffed ourselves, sampling each of the items. I was about to fall into a food coma when someone broke out in song. Soon everyone – from Grandma to the kids – was singing unreservedly. Irina and Nikola rose to dance in a close embrace. I felt like I was on the set of a movie: *My Big Fat Macedonian Easter*. My family at home never broke out in heartfelt song and dance at holiday meals. A spike of jealousy shot through me at the exuberant outpouring of familial love even though our hosts regarded us as part of the family.

My own family didn't hug or kiss or sing or dance. We didn't even drink. Bickering, snide remarks, and leaving as soon as possible after eating were our holiday traditions. Other than anger, we didn't express any emotions. Especially not love. Ew. Recently my mother commented that no one could have loved their children more than she loved me and my sister. I was dumbfounded. She loved us? Where were the hugs and kisses, the empathetic ear, the concern for our emotional lives? She wanted to make us good, not happy. I knew she loved us on some level, but it never occurred to me that she could feel the same consuming love for me that I felt for my children. It kind of freaked me out.

Little did I know that my own stiff, WASPy family was about to become a Lifetime movie, and not one with a happy ending.

Although I was enjoying Macedonia, I was worried because my father had begun to lose his mind. Not in a dementia kind of way, but in a have-you-lost-your-damn-mind kind of way. Four months previously, Dad asked me to meet him at a McDonald's near my parents' home. Mystified, I agreed, worried he was going to tell me he had cancer. My father was a seventy-one-year-old teetotaling Sunday School teacher and church deacon who was coming up on his fiftieth year of marriage to my mother. We ordered milkshakes, and he explained his dilemma.

"I've started talking to my old high school girlfriend on Facebook," he confessed. "Should I tell Mom about it?"

"Duh," I replied and stifled a laugh, relieved that he wasn't dying. "Where does this woman live?"

"California."

Truly nothing to worry about then. "Is she married?"

"Yeah, to a dentist."

I went home and told Craig the big secret. We had a good chuckle.

My dad did tell Mom about contacting his old girlfriend, but communication with his old flame increased. My mother and the woman have the same first name which only added to the weirdness. By Easter my dad was yammering on about how "spring was the time for love." In front of my mother. While my father has always played the comedian, a seventy-year-old acting like an amorous teenager was not amusing. He didn't seem to understand that proclaiming his love for another woman in front of my mother was not comical.

"I hope you have a brain tumor," I told him. "Because I can't think of any other excuse for this insanity." Perhaps he didn't find that amusing either. My father suffering from a serious illness was no longer the worst crisis I could think of.

As I watched Irina and Nikola dancing in their cramped dining room, I envied their intimacy, of the evidence of romance still alive and well after decades of marriage. Irina was a bot-tle-blonde with green eyes and a gap in her teeth. Nikola was short and squat with salt and pepper hair and an admirable mustache. There were parallels between the Petrovskis and the LaVentures: the driven, workaholic wives of academia and the laid-back, hard-drinking husbands. Like us, the Petrovskis had a first-born son and a second-born daughter, even though their children were a few years older than ours. Peter and Vicki visited their parents in North Carolina but returned home to continue their studies at the University in Skopje. There were differences between our families, as well. Irina was a more traditional wife and mother than I, catering to Nikola and her children in addi-tion to pursuing professional endeavors. Unlike me, she seemed to hold no animosity about the inequitable distribution of the workload in her marriage. Seeing her prepare the Easter feast, I was impressed with her positive attitude while performing "womanly duties." Vicki helped with lunch and she and her brother participated enthusiastically in the post-lunch singalong. I couldn't imagine my teenage children willingly helping or sing-ing. The effusive familial love I witnessed at the Petrovskis' home was almost too much for me to take. My lifelong habit of earning tokens of love through achievement couldn't process this unconditional love and approval.

After our extravagant feast, we strolled the streets of Ohrid, attempting to work off lunch. We passed statues of Saints Cyril and Methodius, brothers and missionaries to the Slavs who invented the Glagolitic alphabet, used as the basis for Russian and other Slavic languages. Another statue depicted one of their disciples: Saint Kliment, the patron saint of Ohrid, Macedonia, and the Macedonian Orthodox Church. Peering over Kliment's statue, we glimpsed the only bit of Americana we saw there: the Golden Arches of St. Mickey D. There was a terrible Irish pub with a shamrock on the wall, but not a drop of Guinness to be found. Families enjoyed the holiday afternoon around the lake; a row of tricked-out tricycles looking like tiny ATVs lined the sidewalk.

Back at our hotel, I began to worry about the workshop sessions I was set to give starting the next day. I was intimidated about teaching university professors. Most of my grad school friends had completed their PhDs and taught at universities. I sensed they felt sorry for me for teaching at a community college. I had been automatically placed into the PhD program based on my master's qualifying exams, but I hadn't wanted to stay in Illinois for three more years. Seth had graduated, it was cold and boring, and academia carried an air of fakery and snobbery I couldn't tolerate even though I made perfect grades. I enjoyed Spanish Literature, but I couldn't pretend it *mattered* when children in the world were starving. Also, I enjoyed teaching the beginning levels of Spanish, and nothing I learned in a PhD program was going to help with that. Sometimes I think about where my path would have led if I'd obtained a doctoral degree, but I can't say I regret my decision. None of my friends with PhDs had been invited to give a workshop in Macedonia for a week.

Still, the stigma loomed large in my mind, so I prepared like crazy for my sessions, including reading a full-length textbook on intercultural communication. I learned so much: monochronous vs. polychronous views of time, hierarchical vs. egalitarian structures, low vs. high context communication, the distinction between values, norms, and worldviews. The famous iceberg analogy of culture stuck with me: the things we often label as cultural differences are literally the tip of the iceberg. Much more lies under the surface – notions of modesty, concepts of beauty, attitudes toward aging and death, approaches to decision making, and much, much more. This was the point where I began to study culture at every opportunity. I had experienced many cultures; now I wanted to better understand what I had experienced. I'd felt the magic of intercultural encounters; now I wanted to know the science behind it.

On Monday morning, we traveled two hours north to a ski resort in Mavrovo. The ski season had ended, and we had the entire creepy hotel to ourselves. The town seemed empty, and a beautiful but eerie church sat half-submerged in a lake at the bottom of the hill. Taxidermied bears, deer, and foxes decorated the lodge. Live peacocks and bunnies roamed in a glassed-in courtyard. Two large dogs were chained outside. Here was a culture clash: Macedonians believe dogs have a job (guarding the property) and have no qualms about leaving them chained up all day and night. During one of my lectures about American culture, they could not believe that Craig drives our dog to the vineyard sometimes because "she wants to go for a ride."

Vinnie and I tag-teamed workshop sessions. The presentation of mine they liked best was "Things Americans Love" (ice, ranch dressing, guns, the flag, sweatpants, musical theater, eating while driving, football, pets, God, wearing pajamas in public, and toilet paper, to name a few.) They also enjoyed "A Day in My Life" in which I showed them photos from a typical weekday, many of which made them giggle—from a bleary-eyed selfie when I awoke, to Craig driving Anna to the end of the driveway to catch the school bus, to the students in my Spanish classroom, to my clumsy moves in Zumba class. I also gave some more academic presentations, but learning should be fun. The workshop was Macedonian paced: We started late in the morning, took a long lunch with wine, and were done by five in the afternoon each day. In the evening, we dined as a group in the hotel's restaurant.

One night Vinnie put us to work, and we made an Indian feast in the hotel kitchen. After dinner, the entire group headed to the basement where a swimming pool and sauna awaited. As soon as we took a seat in the sauna, the Macedonian professors broke out into an exuberant song. No surprise there, though I've never participated in a singalong while wrapped in a nothing but a towel with my American colleagues. Macedonians share true affection for one another and welcome visitors in a way I've never seen matched. They spend inordinate amounts of time eating, drinking, and singing. After ten days of endless food, drink and relaxation, I was ready to get home and start accomplishing things. My fingers itched for a good, sharp pencil to cross items off a list. Craig would have stayed there forever, but I am not good at relaxing. Constantly doing keeps my low buzz of discontent at inaudible levels.

On the other hand, I wasn't anxious to get home where I'd have to deal with my parents' romantic tragedy. The month I returned from Macedonia, my father's girlfriend flew to North Carolina so they could see each other in person. Mom was hoping a face-to-face encounter between two senior citizens would put out the fire. It didn't. Mom told Dad he had to choose between her and his Facebook honey, an ultimatum he found shocking. He didn't understand why he couldn't live at home and keep his California girlfriend on the side. Begrudgingly, he moved out, taking his collection of 80,000 comic books with him in his fifteen-passenger van. My parents obtained a permanent legal separation, a legal option in North Carolina that's cheaper than a divorce but more final than a regular separation. My dad's girlfriend moved to North Carolina, and they share a townhome. She's still married to her California husband. In fact, she and my father flew to California to house sit for J2's hubby while he attended a college reunion. Her husband has also planned vacations for his wife and my father. WTF?

My father didn't see why I was taking this so hard.

"Geez, you're almost fifty years old. People get divorced," he told me. "Why are you being so judgy?"

My head did not explode though I thought it might.

"How many people leave their wives after almost fifty years of marriage for an old girlfriend they hooked up with on Facebook?" I countered.

Apparently, more than I thought.

He wouldn't acknowledge that his actions flew in the face of everything he'd taught me all his life: Marriage is a sacrament, a lifelong commitment, a pact between a couple and God. He couldn't see his decision was an asteroid blowing a chunk out of my mental world. I always idolized my dad and was proud to be just like him. I could not fathom that he had done this. I knew men did this kind of thing all the time, but not *my dad*. He was the fun parent, a silly man who entertained my friends with his jokes and physical comedy. Once when he dropped me off at a sleepover, he drove up and down the road with his leg out the window as the other little girls stood in the yard and shrieked with laughter and disbelief. He never drank, never cheated, rarely raised his voice.

My sister wasn't nearly as shocked as I was. Cindy knew his Peter Pan persona made him capable of such a thing.

Dad didn't understand that the immorality of his actions wasn't about what he was doing with the new (old) woman, but about what he was doing to my mother (the *old* old woman). I'd rarely seen my mother cry in my nearly fifty years of life, now she cried every day. She also called me daily, talking nonstop for an hour, often repeating what she'd said the day before. I tried to get her to see a counselor, find a friend, or get a pet. I was so busy with work and kids I barely had a spare moment. Even though she was the wronged party, it was a stressful and unpleasant obligation to have to listen to her badmouth my father every day for an hour. She'd get mad if she could hear me unloading the dishwasher or performing any other task, so I'd often put the phone on speaker and mute. She didn't need me to say anything apparently; she just needed my full listening attention. Being in Macedonia had been a nice break from the daily phone calls.

I tried not to dwell on what was to come as the van drove us through the night to the airport in Skopje. The evening before, we bid fond farewells to all our Macedonian friends at the end of the workshop. Now we were flying home from the country's capital and birthplace of Mother Teresa. I knew what this modern saint thought of people with leprosy ("Christ in his most distressing disguise"), but what would she think of my father? Was forgiveness an injustice in this situation? How could I forgive my father without absolving him? It would take several years for me to come to a place of peace about his actions. One of Mother Teresa's quotes came to me in the darkness as we drove toward the airport: "What can you do to promote world peace? Go home and love your family." Her fellow Macedonians seemed to be doing a great job of it. We Americans could learn a lot from them.

My friend Susan had stayed with our kids while we were gone. At thirteen and sixteen, Anna and Daniel were good kids and largely self-sufficient, but they still required adult supervision. I greeted my precious babies with big hugs and many kisses. They tolerated it before asking the most American of questions: "What'd ya bring us?" A renewed commitment to expressing my profound and unconditional love for them while being nicer to their father?

They preferred the gifts from my suitcase, but that's okay. I could give them both.

AUSTRALIA & NEW ZEALAND: THE WEEK WITHOUT A TUESDAY

Following a three-hour flight from Charlotte to Dallas, I boarded a sixteen-hour flight to Brisbane, Australia, with five other adult travelers. It was Monday evening, and I popped a pill and settled in for what I hoped would be a long nap. I'm a terrible plane sleeper, but I'm hesitant to take enough drugs to knock me out when I'm leading a group of students in case someone needs me. I figured my all-adult group would be fine without me being fully conscious. On Wednesday morning, we landed in Australia. What the heck happened to Tuesday? We had traveled into the future, crossing the International Date Line and moving from Monday to Wednesday with nary a trace of Tuesday.

Heading Down Under is the Mount Everest of flying. Careful preparation and dedication are required to avoid dehydration, desperation, and desolation before reaching the destination. The flight from Dallas to Brisbane was in the top ten longest flights of 2014, covering over eight thousand miles in sixteen hours. Qantas is a great airline, which is akin to saying it's like the vestibule of Hell instead of one of the lower circles. Despite the eye masks and toothbrushes and snack bar and sleeping pills and attractive flight attendants with cute accents, it was still a freaking long time on a plane. It felt like three days.

A non-plane-sleeper must be a masochist to attempt a twelve-day trip to Australia *and* New Zealand, so naturally this was the tour I chose. I thought New Zealand was right next to Australia, so it was a shock when we stumbled off the plane in Brisbane only to discover we had another three-and-a-half-hour flight to Auckland, a mere 1500 miles away. By the time we landed in New Zealand, my body and brain were in a time-traveling trance. A giant dwarf statue greeted me in the airport, and I offered it a hallucinatory smile. Welcome to Middle-earth! Although I was mostly over my Orlando Bloom obsession, I still loved *The Lord of the Rings* and the trilogy had been filmed in New Zealand.

A lot had happened in the four years since I became Director of International Education. We were hosting international students and Fulbright Foreign Language Teaching Assistants. Our study abroad opportunities were growing. Each semester I created and oversaw a series of over thirty passport events, cultural talks and international presentations open to faculty, staff, and students. We'd created a Scholars of Global Distinction program for domestic students to earn an award on their transcripts that indicated they'd taken internationalized courses, attended passport events, and had a global experience (study abroad or a 30-hour domestic experience with an international component.) We even won the 2014 institutional award for exemplary and outstanding international programming from the North Carolina Association of International Educators, a prize most often awarded to universities. I was working hard and getting noticed. Daniel had left for college and Anna was a self-sufficient junior in high school. I threw myself into my job, my passion for international education intertwining with my love for achievement into a whirlwind of constant activity that left no time for contemplating my impending empty nest.

The most fun development was the creation of the Community Travel Club, which was formed in 2013 to celebrate the college's 50th anniversary. The college president believed a community travel experience to Switzerland and Italy would be a wonderful way to promote lifelong learning and community engagement. She, her husband, and a dozen other prominent community members signed up for the ten-day trip. At first, I was worried that traveling with wealthy grownups might prove more difficult than managing students, but that was a misplaced fear. All were seasoned travelers – culturally competent, gracious and uncomplaining. Our guide was a beautiful man named Osciri. We were all smitten with his blue eyes and black hair which he pulled back into a thick ponytail. He sported a perfect five o'clock shadow throughout the entire day. Gracious, helpful, and informative, Osciri had the ladies of the group enthralled and the men slightly infatuated as well. From important historical information to juicy tidbits about Berlusconi's bunga bunga sex parties with Libyan leader Muammar Gaddafi, Osciri informed and entertained in equal measure. Best. Tour. Guide. Ever.

The travel club members indicated interest in a tour to Australia the following year, but none of them except Craig's friend Brandt ended up being able to go. Our Down Under group consisted of me, my friend Susan, Brandt, and three other older women. Since there were just six of us, the tour company combined us with a couple of other groups, including a loud bunch of college kids from Florida. Why is it always Florida? Mel, our tour director, met us in the terminal. She resembled Mick Jagger in her severe thinness and the rock-and-roll lines on her face. Throughout the tour she regaled us with stories of her groupie days. A Kiwi by birth (born in New Zealand), she taught us to use the Māori greeting "Kia Ora!" but forgot to tell us much else. I couldn't figure out if her brain was drug-addled or if she had led so many tours that she couldn't remember what she'd already told us or didn't care. She was no Osciri.

I had turned fifty a few months previously, and I was feeling it. The long flights and time difference left me tired and bad-tempered. I was also cranky about my weight gain. I had lost ninety pounds in 2010-2011 and had slowly been gaining it back. For fourteen months I had been "perfect," following the Weight Watcher guidelines meticulously and losing weight every week without a single plateau or bad week. Don't tell me I don't have willpower. For more than a year, I tracked everything I put into my mouth, including Communion wafers, Altoids, and the cream in my coffee. Constant hunger became my norm. When my stomach wasn't growling, I worried I wasn't losing weight. If I planned on drinking a glass of wine, I made sure to burn off the calories in advance on the elliptical machine. I lifted weights and did Zumba five or six days a week, sometimes doing back-to-back classes.

To my future remorse, I posted weekly on Facebook about my weight loss, including before and after photos. The response was tremendous. Everyone loves a loser (when it comes to weight). So much positive affirmation for my achievement. You would have thought I invented a cure for cancer considering all the accolades that poured in. Being praised for my accomplishment fed into my need to earn love through doing extraordinary things. Controlling my body felt like mastering the universe. I sauntered into department stores into the sections for "regular" sized people, glancing around to make sure no salesperson was approaching to point me to the plus-sized clothing.

At a size eight, I still felt fat. According to whoever creates those ridiculous charts, I was *barely* in the normal weight range for my height. My skin sagged and I did not look good naked as I had hoped. Corporations spend billions making sure women don't feel satisfied with their faces and bodies. The diet industry has us all chasing carrots that are just out of reach. I have yet to meet a woman who is happy with her body. Never mind that my body has carried me around the world, produced two children, and allowed me to dance, swim, walk, play, and rest. It didn't look like an airbrushed supermodel's body. Worst of all, after I reached my goal, the applause died down.

Shortly after hitting my lowest weight, I attended a conference in California. I took my window seat on the plane, accustomed to trying to squeeze myself into the smallest amount of space possible. A man sat next to me in the middle seat.

"Thanks for being small," this total stranger said to me as way of introduction.

I couldn't understand his words for several seconds. Finally, I responded.

"Oh, I'm not small. I'm a fat person in disguise. I just lost ninety pounds."

He didn't speak to me for the rest of the flight, thank goodness. I could only think of all the times I'd flown when I wasn't small and what people must have been thinking about having to sit next to me. I'd always felt self-conscious about flying, about my child-birthing hips lapping over my assigned seat area, and this douchebag confirmed my worst fears.

Gaining the weight back was the worst feeling in the world. The shame was overwhelming, especially since I made such a public spectacle of my weight loss. It was like sliding down a cliff trying to dig my fingernails into the rocky wall to slow my fall. Over and over, I would attempt to get back on the wagon. I would toe the line, count my points, do Zumba every day, and still, I didn't lose weight. By the 2014 trip to Australia, I had put back on thirty pounds, which still left me down sixty. But rather than be happy that I was still in non-plus-size clothing, I was miserable. It would take me years and many scientific studies to accept what I should have known through experience: Diets don't work. They slow your metabolism and teach your body to become extremely efficient at holding onto weight. Chronic dieting makes your body think you are trying to kill it so it does everything it can to prevent that. Your brain sends out all kinds of signals and produces hormones encouraging you to return to your former size. 95 percent of people who lose weight gain it back, but doctors continue to prescribe this treatment that has a 5 percent success rate. But in 2014, I was still buying into diet culture which considers being overweight to be a moral flaw. The thunderous acclamation for my weight loss had turned into a deafening silence with an occasional rude remark from acquaintances if I was observed eating something other than chicken or lettuce. I was in a constant shame-fueled bad mood, which couldn't be lifted by the achievement of checking off my sixth continent.

★ ★ ★

It was nighttime when we checked into a Best Western in Auckland, on New Zealand's North Island. Susan and I stumbled outside the hotel and walked around the block in a daze, grabbing a bottle of water and a snack at a convenience store. Early the next morning, the bus whisked us away to Rotorua, where we learned about Māori culture and observed the geothermal baths. Is it terrible that I was comforted by the fact that many of the Māori people aren't small? I felt a kinship with them, unlike many of the rail-thin Europeans I'd met. We visited Whakarewarewa, which advertises itself as "the living Māori village." We learned how they used natural geothermal resources to cook, bathe, and heat their homes. We traipsed down boardwalks through bubbling mud pits and steaming pools reeking of sulfur. They reminded me of the dead marshes from *LOTR*, and I peered in attempting to see the ghostly faces

of long-dead men and elves. Our guides were friendly, descendants of the Tūhourangi Ngāti Wāhiao people, complete with the
iconic face tattoos Harvey Keitel sported in *The Piano*. I had
seen the film when I was six months pregnant with Daniel and
the movie left me disturbed for days.

"Are your face tattoos real?" I asked our guide.

"No, this is a side gig. I work full-time at the local auto
parts store."

That bummed me out, but I enjoyed the vigorous warrior greeting we received upon arrival. Haka is traditionally
performed when preparing for battle (or a rugby match) and
involves a lot of chanting, foot-stomping, eye-bulging, and
tongue-protruding. It was simultaneously comical and terrifying. I was glad I wasn't facing them in battle. Following our
fearsome welcome, we enjoyed an authentic Hāngi dinner where
baskets of meat, potatoes, and vegetables were cooked in a pit
full of hot stones covered with earth. The meal was followed by
a song-and-dance show that reminded me of a Hawaiian luau.
It was entertaining, but had a cheesy, touristy feel. I felt sad that
Indigenous people had to pimp out their culture as a side hustle.
How can people share their culture in a dignified and authentic
way? I often wonder if my tourism dollars are helping or hurt-
ing, so I make every attempt to have more than a superficial
knowledge about the people and places I visit. Our study abroad
committee continuously works on our improving the study
abroad class participant take before traveling. Maximizing the
development of cultural competence is the goal, with an emphasis on meaningful reflection on the experience.

I was not a model participant on the Australia-New Zealand
trip. A black cloud of weight gain failure and shame trailed me.
I had little interest in the activities geared to traditionally-aged
college students: an amphibious duck tour, a sheep show, rolling down a hill in a big, inflated ball, riding a luge down a

mountain. Actually, the sheep show was great, and Susan and I had fun on the luge, but it was all a preamble to the only thing I wanted to see in New Zealand: Hobbiton!

Visiting the filming location for the Shire in *The Lord of the Rings* was the one thing that lifted my mood. I know I just complained about a tourist site replicating an Indigenous culture and I've expressed my profound disdain for Disney World. However, I had no qualms about paying a hundred bucks to visit a made-up place where an imaginary group of diminutive, hairy-footed, mushroom-loving, pipe-weed-smoking hobbits lived. I gazed upon the party tree where Bilbo Baggins celebrated his eleventy-first birthday and then shocked the crowd by mysteriously disappearing. I stared into the sky where Gandalf thrilled the crowd with fireworks of flying dragons. I posed in the doorway of Frodo's and Sam's hobbit holes. Susan and Molly and I drank a pint at the Green Dragon by the fire.

They tore down the Shire set after they filmed *The Lord of the Rings* and rebuilt it for the Hobbit movies. I hate the Hobbit movies. They violate all that is sacred and make me barf. The Hobbit movies should be thrown into the cracks of Mt. Doom and destroyed along with the ring. Saruman should toss the Hobbit movies off the tower of Orthanc. Shelob should plunge her poisonous stinger deep within the films until they die. The Witch King of Angmar should feed the Hobbit movies to the fell beasts of the Nazgûl. Sauron should incinerate them with his lidless eye. In case I haven't made myself clear, I'm not a huge fan of the Hobbit movies. However, being in Hobbiton filled me with the kind of joy a hobbit feels when offered a pint, a feast, a pipe, a chat with friends by the fire. I was happy in the Shire.

Having experienced my personal highlight of the trip, I settled in for the rest of the tour, which was in Australia. I didn't like Australia. I didn't hate it like I hate the Hobbit movies, but it's near the bottom of my list of places I've visited. Australia is super expensive, and I tend not to like any place where things cost more than they do at home. Twenty-five bucks for a hamburger? No, thanks. There's not a lot of unique Australian cuisine. You can order a kangaroo burger, but why? Then there's vegemite, a yeast-based spread with an allegedly indescribable taste. Pass. Australia does have delicious chocolate-covered cookies called Tim Tams. I loaded my suitcase with them (the grocery store is a wonderful place to buy cheap gifts) only to discover I could buy them at my local World Market. I splurged and bought Anna a pair of real Ugg's which fell apart within months to the dismay of both of us. We saw kangaroos and koalas in a couple of mini zoos. But nothing in Australia sparked joy in me.

The food wasn't vastly different, the language wasn't different, the culture wasn't different. Why the hell did I fly halfway around the world to a place that's just like Canada? In addition to my weight-gaining shame, I was jaded from traveling. We visited the Sydney Tower, the world's seventh tallest building; in Shanghai three years previously, I'd been to the top of the Shanghai Financial Center, the world's second tallest building. We took a harbor cruise, and I snapped photos of the Opera House and the Harbor Bridge, but I'd already taken river or harbor cruises in Paris, New York, Budapest, Seattle, and Toronto, to name a few. On this trip, all I could think was *been there, done that.* This was unusual for me. Normally, travel was an instant cure for my recurring ennui. I felt guilty about my jadedness, and hoped this was a temporary mood.

Travel was the life-giving juice to fuel my regular life: hard-working wife, devoted mother, loyal daughter, dedicated employee, community volunteer, faithful Christian. Experiencing other places a few times a year undergirded my day-to-day life. In addition to international travel, my schedule now included multiple national conferences each year, so I traversed the U.S. as well as the globe. From Seattle to D.C. to Los Angeles to Orlando, I hit all the major cities.

There's nothing I love more than a hotel room by myself. A little alone time every few months with no laundry or family or students demanding my immediate attention was such a relief. I enjoyed meals and drinks with my colleagues and didn't even mind presenting three or four times at a single conference but being alone in a hotel room with no one needing me was heaven. There was nothing to prove or achieve, no need to perform or hold my tongue. I was never bored, never lonely, never dissatisfied when I had a room of my own.

Except for the day in Hobbiton, the *blahs* plagued me throughout Australia and New Zealand. I had to laugh at my jadedness when they took us to a jade factory in Rotorua. We watched a craftsman carve the green gemstone as he explained the different symbols used in jewelry. Then we were released into the attached store to shop. I stood outside while the busload of students loaded up on souvenirs. It's not unusual for tours to contain cultural excursions which are thinly disguised shopping trips. I don't know the details of the kickbacks tour companies get for bringing large groups of eager customers to these sites, but there's definitely some kind of commission. In Sydney, we visited the National Opal Collection which was pretty much the same deal. I caved and bought a cheap pair of opal earrings in the airport on the way home, but one of the opals promptly fell out of the setting and I never bothered to repair it.

Our last three-night stay in Australia was in Cairns, a beach town with a cool night market. I struggled with pronouncing the name of the city. The Australians all pronounced it "Cans", but I think that's because they don't pronounce their Rs. I was worried if I pronounced it like the Aussies, it would sound like I was making fun of their accent but that if I pronounced it American style, they would think I was stupid. God knows I can't stand for anyone to think I'm stupid.

I *was* looking forward to our excursion to the Great Barrier Reef from Cairns; I'd never been anywhere like that before. Unfortunately, it too, was a bust. The day was cool and blustery day as we boarded the cruise. The large boat held multiple levels and hundreds of people. A lot of the tourists were Asian, which shouldn't have surprised me since Asia is just north of Australia. In fact, Indonesia is much closer to Cairns than New Zealand is to Sydney. (Sometimes my own lack of geographical proficiency makes me feel stupid.)

Mel, our tour guide, paced nervously as we settled in on various decks.

"Water looks rough," she muttered. We soon discovered how rough.

Maybe you've heard of mass hysteria? What about mass vomiting? People started upchucking ten minutes into the trip. I lay still on a bench with my eyes closed, trying to catch some whiffs of salt air from the cloud of barf. I was glad I didn't have any young students I was compelled to check on. Mel's hardcore background as a groupie seemed to keep her immune from puking. Of course, she didn't eat much, so maybe there wasn't anything in her stomach to be ejected. Finally, after an interminable hour, we stopped and dropped anchor. Slowly, the green faces turned back to their normal color. When the crew called for people to put on wetsuits and jump into the murky water, only a handful of people participated. Molly, a woman a few years older than me, enthusiastically headed for the water while the rest of us looked at her disbelievingly but not without admiration. Molly had a fantastic time which did put a faint smile on my face.

I had already been iffy about putting on a wetsuit in front of others and attempting to snorkel. The one time I tried snorkeling in Mexico wasn't great. I'm not a strong swimmer, and I'm also too uncoordinated to figure out how to breathe in air and not water. My brain tried to convince myself: This is the only chance I'll ever have to see the Great Barrier Reef. My stomach responded: You better sit the hell back down. I settled for taking a ride in the glassed-in submersible, but all I could see were a couple of fish swimming by. The crew laid out an elaborate lunch buffet which few people touched. Two-thirds of the passengers sat, waiting to go home, while one-third engaged in snorkeling.

As we cruised back to land, I mulled over my Australian experience. Checking off my sixth continent *was* cool. Perhaps a longer, slower exploration of the country would be nice. Ayers Rock and the Outback might be fun—except for the giant spiders and deadly vipers stalking the interior of the country. Maybe I was too old for educational tours designed to keep teenagers exhausted and occupied at every moment. In fact, this turned out to be the last program I led with a massive educational travel company. I wasn't done with adventure, but it was taking a turn.

On our return to the States, we had four flights totaling thirty-six hours of travel. We departed from the northeast coast of Australia on Friday morning and after four flights arrived in North Carolina the same evening, in time to see fourth of July fireworks below us from the windows of the plane. I traded the Tuesday I missed for an extended Friday. Regardless, I was happy to be home. Perhaps it's just my oppositional nature that caused me to dislike Australia. Maybe my impending empty nest status was an underlying cause of my angst. If travel could no longer fill up my empty spaces, I guess I just needed to work harder.

CHINA: THERE AND BACK AGAIN

On a sweltering July day, the college president ushers me into her office for a meeting with Wayne, the Director of International Programs for the American Association of Community Colleges. By 2015, our college was gaining a national reputation for our international education program. We were the only community college in the country to reach our Generation Study Abroad goal to double the number of participants in study abroad in the first year of the initiative along with eleven four-year universities. We couldn't afford to send anyone to accept the award since community college resources pale in comparison with four-year schools. At that time in North Carolina, the fifty-eight community colleges in the state educated three times the number of students as the sixteen public universities on one-third as much money from the public education budget. In other words, a community college student receives about 11 percent of the taxpayer money that a university student does.

Wayne is a colleague I met through CCID – Community Colleges for International Development. He attended our SIO (Senior International Officer) meetings held at the annual conference and at the summer board meeting. He's friendly, but formal, with short-cropped hair and rimless glasses. He's impeccably dressed as always despite the heat.

"Hi, Suzanne," he greets me. "I was just talking about our upcoming delegation to China. I'd love for you to join us. We'll be presenting at the China Annual Conference for International Education and making site visits to potential partners."

"Suzanne would be happy to represent the college in China," the president says.

"Yes, of course," I reply. "That would be fantastic."

Oh crap, I think as I smile. This is my life now—show up to work on a slow summer day and go home with a plane ticket to Beijing and a conference presentation to prepare for a Chinese audience. Who could have imagined that my path would lead here?

I like Wayne and normally I am excited to go anywhere. My ennui from the Australia trip had receded and I never say no to an opportunity. But China—again? My first trip to China in 2011 had been fantastic. Chinese people are unfailingly kind and gracious. I thought I might lose weight while there, but I gained three pounds from the delicious and healthy cuisine. China has the oldest living civilization in the world, the only ancient culture that still exists. While the United States is less than 300 years old, written Chinese history has existed for more than 4000 years. We are a baby culture, and it shows in comparison. The Chinese name for China is Zhōngguó, which can be translated as the Middle Kingdom, probably because they considered themselves to be at the center of the world. While Americans are widely known for our ethnocentrism, China may be right about their centrality in global importance. With thousands of years of history, the world's second largest population, the most spoken first language, the fastest growing and second-largest economy, China is not a country to ignore.

Let me explain my hesitation about a return visit: It had little to do with communism or human rights violations or religious repression or even my own jadedness. A government is a temporary thing; it does not define people or culture or history.

My overwhelming preoccupation was the lack of coffee and toilets. Both can be hard to find in the Middle Kingdom. When I was younger, these wouldn't have mattered so much. And yes, I would use the toilet less often if I didn't drink coffee, but I am too old and my thighs are too flabby to learn how to squat effectively over a drain in the floor. I am also too old and tired to not drink coffee. Not having coffee is compounded by not having sleep. The mattress in the dorm on my first trip was an actual wooden plank. I'm not Princess-and-the-Pea sensitive, but I don't understand the concept of intentionally sleeping on a rock-hard slab. The Chinese say it's good for your back, but I have never been highly motivated by what's good for me. To take cultural differences a step further, dairy products are virtually non-existent in China (Asian populations tend to be lactose intolerant.) I can live without cheese if I must, but why would I want to? Cheese is a cornerstone on my personal food pyramid. And what's cheese without a nice cabernet or malbec? Another thing I didn't see much of on my first visit.

Of course, I would never complain about any of these things out loud while in China. The combination of international travel, conferences, webinars, and independent study taught me a lot about culture. One thing I've learned is that culture is *embodied*: just because I *know* China is a tea culture and that squat toilets are common does not mean I will stop craving coffee and suddenly become proficient at—well, squatting. Culture competence means respecting the rules, norms, and practices in another country which differ from your own. It doesn't mean that you will be able to shed your own culture like a snakeskin and pull on a different one. It doesn't mean you'll stop wishing for a toilet, but you do need to keep your negative thoughts to yourself. Occasionally, a cultural difference will strike you as a great idea. For example, most Chinese people shower at night to wash away the dirt from the outside world and so they're clean when they put on their pajamas and get in the bed. Makes sense to me.

On my first trip to China, I accompanied a group of students and faculty from four different community colleges. I was thrilled to go and not just so I could take a selfie on the Great Wall and cross off Asia from my list of continents. The students were pumped, and it was fun to watch them even though I winced as they shouted *xie xie* to everyone they met. None of them pronounced it the same way or had any concept of what a tonal language is. Who knows if the Chinese understood anything they said. Another cultural difference is that in China people don't say "thank you" in every other sentence like we are trained to do. A Chinese woman who gives you change in the store has no idea why you would thank her for handing you coins that belong to you. What would be rude in our culture isn't in theirs.

Mandarin is the most widely spoken first language in the world. It's also the only language I've found impenetrable. I tried to learn a few phrases as I always do but felt zero confidence in my ability to accurately say anything other than "*ni hao.*" If I'm afraid to speak Spanish after decades of study, there's no way I'm attempting to speak Mandarin to native speakers despite my normal practice of learning a bit of the language before I travel anywhere. The U.S. State Department classifies Mandarin as one of the hardest languages for English speakers to learn, requiring 2200 hours of study to achieve proficiency. It doesn't have an alphabet; just thousands of characters that don't even represent words per se, but rather "meaningful forms." Then there's the fact that every syllable can be pronounced differently using five different tones. And then there's the cultural aspect of language: While Americans are a low context culture, China is a high context culture. Americans lay it out straight, we say what we mean and mean what we say, straight to the point. In

Chinese culture, the actual words are far less important than the context in which they're spoken. And learning contextual language clues is even more difficult than learning the language itself. I have a tough time being indirect, to the point of lacking tact. Not being straightforward feels like lying to me, though I understand that sometimes kindness is more important than truth. Like my mama taught me, you don't have to say everything you think. Holding my tongue has always been a struggle for me.

One morning after our lecture about healthcare, a group of Chinese students from our partner university in Beijing accompanied us to the Forbidden City. We were amazed to learn that none of these students knew about the pro-democracy protests and massacre that had occurred at Tiananmen Square in 1989. It was hard to believe a government could keep a billion people in the dark about something thousands had witnessed first-hand. I was using a VPN to access Facebook in China, but it was incredible to me that university students had no knowledge of one of the 20th century's most famous events which had happened in their own city. Censorship of information, suppression of religious freedom, and an emphasis on conformity are all a part of modern China.

Western tourists were not prolific and when we stopped at the Tiananmen gate to take selfies with the famous portrait of Mao, random Chinese people asked to take pictures with us, especially with the blonde and Black students. Isaiah was maybe six-foot-two, but the Chinese seemed to think he was an NBA player, and he didn't correct them. He basked in the glory of being famous, posing happily with all who asked. Isaiah was from a community college in Oklahoma and his faculty leader was Tony. Another part of our group was led by Nadine, from a large urban community college down the road from my school. After our adventure in China, Nadine became one of my dearest and bestest friends. In addition to regular phone chats, we've traveled together to Guatemala, Ireland, Qatar, South Africa, and Mexico as well as all across the United States for conferences. Nadine has a hilarious video of us in the back of a cab in San Miguel de Allende documenting the day we skipped an afternoon of conference sessions and visited a deserted, semi run-down spa. We giggled about the sketchy resort, where we splashed alone in leaf-filled pools and lounged on moderately clean-looking canopied beds, speculating about who at the conference would notice if we went missing. She replays it whenever she needs a laugh.

Halfway across Tiananmen Square, one of Nadine's students fell out, as we say in the South. This sixty-year-old man (community college students come in all shapes and sizes and ages) collapsed on the sidewalk and was taken to the hospital. Nadine and Tony and I took turns staying with him over the next week, a bit shocked when we saw his shirtless torso marked with a couple of old bullet scars and stab wounds. Apparently, he ate something on the plane that disagreed with him, so he had decided not to eat or drink anything for the next few days. (General life tip: you must eat and drink to stay alive.)

After a week in Beijing ("old China"), we boarded an overnight train to Shanghai ("new China"), where we listened to a lecture on the differences between Eastern and Western perspectives. The professor showed us a painting and gave us a few seconds to record what we saw on a slip of paper. Most of us answered "Tigers." I was extremely proud that my answer was "Three tigers on a rock in the snow," demonstrating that I could think in the Eastern way, where background was as important as foreground. Of course, one of my students answered "Lions," thus perpetuating the community college stigma. The concept that there is a whole other way of thinking fascinates me. Neuroimaging studies have shown that the medial prefrontal cortex of a Chinese person thinking about their mother lights up as if they were thinking about themselves. When Americans think about Mom, their brains react the same as if they were thinking about a stranger. Fascinating.

Other cultural activities included visiting the Shanghai World Financial Center, the second tallest building in the world at that time. From the observation deck on the hundredth floor, we saw much of the city despite the smog. In the evening, we took a cruise on the Huangpu River, the skyscrapers along the shore lit with moving LED displays. We strolled down the Bund, a mile-long walkway alongside the river full of historic buildings and soaring skyscrapers. Nadine and I allowed ourselves to be led down secret back alleys to shop for illegal designer purses. Nadine was a pro at examining the bags, checking seams and stitching and logos. I was along for the ride, enjoying the thrill of illicit activity. On my second trip to China, I bought a Michael Kors tote bag for twenty-five dollars which I suspect might be real. It's held up perfectly for many years. Nadine and I learned the faculty member from Florida encouraged his students to buy fake bags and sell them to pay for their trip. What could we do about it? Dealing with unscrupulous colleagues from other colleges is worse than managing unruly students because you have no authority.

My cheapness is unintentionally effective when it comes to bargaining for purses or other items. I keep insisting I'm not interested (which is true) until they reach a price so low I can't help but buy the item. Haggling is a part of so many cultures, but I hate it. I don't mind paying a reasonable price for something I like, but I hate the idea that I'm paying ten times more than what the seller wants. I made a mistake in a Shanghai market: carrying a Starbucks cup with me while browsing. While I protested that a woman was asking too much for some silk pajamas for my great nieces, she nodded toward my latte and pointed out that I had paid more than that for my coffee. Touché. I had been so happy to see a Starbucks after ten days in China, I would have paid any price for a cup of joe. The coffee shop visit also afforded me the opportunity to perform a bit of helpful English-to-English interpretation. A Russian couple in front of me was attempting to order lattes in English and the Shanghainese employee was responding in broken English. Neither could understand the other, but I was able to figure out what the clients wanted and explain it in a way the barista understood. Even though there are far more native Mandarin speakers in the world, English is the lingua franca, the language of business, technology, and overpriced over-roasted coffee.

My body could have used some coffee when we visited the Great Wall at the Mutianyu section outside of Beijing. Worriedly glancing at the steps winding up the mountain to the watchtower, I bemoaned my lack of caffeine. However, I had just reached my Weight Watchers goal and had taken up Zumba with a passion. Still, I had doubts about climbing 4000+ steps. I began the uphill journey, pausing to "look at nature" when I needed to catch my breath. After close to an hour of climbing, I crested and stood on the wall. I glanced around, panting, more amazed that I had made it than I was to be standing on the Great Wall in that moment. The awe came soon, though, as I strolled up and down, this section originally built 1500 years ago and rebuilt and strengthened a mere 650 years ago. A deep green forest of old pines and juniper trees covered the mountainsides. Walking along the ridge of a mountain range felt like strolling along the spine of a dragon. The ancient stones and bricks trailed into the distance for as far as I could see. A bride in a brilliant red dress posed for photos as I passed. I entered the stone archway of a watchtower and sat in the shade by a window, viewing my surroundings and trying to process that I was on the freaking Great Wall of China. After a period of contemplation, I went back to walking the wall, checking my watch.

"Hey, guys," I yelled, spotting a couple of students, "are y'all about ready to start the climb down?"

"Climb?" They looked puzzled. "We're going to take the cable car back down."

Cable car? How had I missed the cable car??

Aggravated that I had not known about the cable car on the way up, I was still happy to take it down. We exited the car to confront the most aggressive vendors I've encountered in the entire world. After the near spiritual experience of exploring one of the Modern Seven Wonders of the World, you face a sea of people hawking T-shirts and coffee mugs. They surround you and grab onto you to get you to buy something. It's intimidating, especially since Americans are fond of our personal space (embodied culture again). It was a bummer to end such an ethereal experience with such a corporally unpleasant one. The Wall spans thousands of miles, so surely some access spots are less overrun with aggressive salespeople.

My student Matt credits me with "making him go to China and changing his life." Persuasion (aka arm-twisting) is one of my superpowers. Matt was blown away by our time in Beijing and Shanghai on that first trip. An Early College student in my Spanish class, he was originally planning on a career in dentistry. After China and completing his associate's degree, he transferred to a university and spent a year studying abroad in Spain. Wow, a student of mine became fluent in Spanish! He now works in international education, and we see each other at conferences. He's always delighted to see me and gushes about the influence I had on him. There's nothing more gratifying than making a difference in someone's life, not even a big pile of frequent flyer miles and a stack of selfies in iconic locations.

The second time I visited China to join Wayne's delegation, I traveled alone. No group of students and faculty to cushion me; I boarded the plane by myself in Chicago and deplaned by myself in Beijing. Much fatter than on my first Asian adventure, the thirteen-hour flight over the North Pole in a middle seat in the back of the plane was no fun. I slept approximately zero. In my great wisdom, I printed out the name of my hotel in Chinese before I left (a great travel tip when it works). However, when I handed it to the cab driver, he seemed to have no idea what it said. He pulled to the curb and talked to me animatedly in Mandarin. I anxiously tried, without success, to get service on my phone. This went on for twenty minutes or so until he called someone on his phone and took off driving. I had no idea if we were headed to the right place or not. As we raced through Beijing, I could only hope he knew where to go.

After a thirty-minute journey through the dystopian skyscrapers bathed in smog, we arrived at the China National Convention Center Grand Hotel, which is right next to the China National Convention Center. To my great relief, I was at the right place. As I stepped into the fancy lobby, a smell I can only describe as bubble bath floated toward me. That is my biggest memory of that hotel: the smell. They must have pumped it through the air vents as a kind of aromatherapy. It was early evening when I checked in. Once in my room, I took a Tylenol PM and flopped onto the bed, grateful for a real mattress. (Thanks, four-star hotel catering to international guests.) A ringing phone brought me to consciousness. It was housekeeping, wanting to know when they could clean my room. I looked at my phone and gasped. It was one-thirty the following afternoon. I had slept fifteen hours, two nights' sleep in one. I took a quick shower and dressed, heading out to who-knows-where so housekeeping could come in.

The Convention Center sits adjacent to the Olympic Park where the 2008 Summer Olympics were held. I wandered around the huge empty squares, gawking at the National Stadium, also known as the Bird's Nest, where Usain Bolt broke three world records. I passed the Water Cube where Michael Phelps won eight gold medals, the most anyone had won in a single Olympics. I found a Western-style underground mall and wandered through looking at clothes that did not come in my size. In most cities, I would have hopped a cab or the metro to see one of the sites, but I had seen many Beijing highlights on my 2011 trip with students, and my total lack of Mandarin kept me close to the hotel. I felt no fear as I wandered alone, but my aloneness stood out as never before. As a white American in a city of twenty million Chinese, blending in was not an option. Six out of ten people in the world are Asian, but our ethnocentric thinking places Western culture at the center of the universe even though it is a minority philosophy.

On Monday morning I met Wayne and the three other community college representatives from around the U.S. I bonded quickly with the other women: Susan from upstate New York and Hadda from Spokane. We put on our suits and gave a presentation about community colleges at the International Education conference being held next door at the Convention Center. We attended other sessions, listening through provided headphones to the English translation. Many community colleges recruit international students and at that time 31 percent of all international students in the U.S. came from China. However, in a society where the pressure to excel is enormous, community college is a tough sell. Everyone in China wants their kid to go to Harvard.

Community colleges are uniquely American. I've spent a lot of time explaining them to people around the world. In fact, when our delegation visited the U.S. Embassy in Beijing, we spent a lot of time explaining them to the *Americans* who worked there. I guess the Foreign Service doesn't have a lot of community college graduates, but that's a shame. Community colleges were created to democratize higher education, to provide a college experience to all people in even rural areas. In 2015, 42 percent of all undergraduates in the U.S. were enrolled at a community college. People used to believe that an educated workforce made our country stronger. Nowadays, there is a tremendous backlash against higher education. It's hard for me to understand how people believe education is a bad thing. I've always wanted to know everything, and I still do. Curiosity may have killed the cat, but it's essential to a meaningful life as a human.

China is as serious as you can get about higher ed. One of our visits was to CHESICC, an institution under the Chinese Ministry of Education which evaluates credentials and keeps student records. Its database contains over a billion student records including Gaokao results, the national college entrance exam. If you think high stakes testing is an issue in the States, the Gaokao says "Hold my beer." It is an extremely difficult test covering all high school subjects and is the sole metric for determining not only which university one may attend, but also one's major. It is given once a year in June to students graduating from high school. It is extremely competitive and people commonly faint during the nine hours of testing over two-three days. There have even been numerous documented cases of suicide influenced by the pressure from the gaokao. The exam is the sole criterion for admission into tertiary education. If you don't score well enough one year, you can have one more try the next. There is no option in China to 'go back to college' if you don't go straight to university. If you don't get in or you can't attend for some reason, then that's that. The idea that a forty-five-year-old mother of three raises her children and then goes to college is unfathomable. The idea that higher education should be accessible to all is literally a foreign concept.

While visiting the CHESICC offices, I asked to use the bathroom, and a young woman escorted me down the hall. Hoping for a western toilet, I was dismayed to see squatty potties in the stalls. Knees creaking, I lowered my pants, tried to squat and aimed for the white drain in the floor. Unfortunately, I still had not mastered the process, and I managed to pee a little on my left pant leg near the ankle. Damn it! I grabbed a tissue from my purse and dabbed at my pants. Luckily, they were black, and nothing showed, but I worried about smelling like pee. Returning to the meeting, I glared at the men in the room, who didn't have this problem.

The Chinese begin toilet training from birth. Babies don't wear diapers; parents just hold them over the toilet. Or a bush. Or a potted plant. Toddlers wear pants with a slit in them, cute little buttocks showing, so they can go when and where they need to. Considering that my son was authoring five-paragraph essays before he would poop in a toilet, maybe they're onto something.

Despite the one child policy implemented from 1979 to 2015, China's population is greater than that of the United States and Europe combined, only recently surpassed by India as the world's most populous nation. Yet with a few exceptions, like martial arts, cuisine, anime, and K-pop, most Americans seem uninterested in what we could learn from Eastern cultures: an appreciation of complexity, the importance of context, emphasis on the good of the whole group instead of focus on the individual, and respect for the wisdom of the aged, to name a few. We are so imbued with the concept of Western superiority that we fail to imagine that another way of thinking might provide insight into our lives. We are afraid to learn that other ways of being are just as valid as our own.

When I was a child, there was a popular commercial that took place in a Chinese laundry. The owner credited his business success to an "ancient Chinese secret," though his wife outed him to a customer declaring Calgon detergent to be the true secret to their success. Though the commercial is now considered racist, I left China believing that the Middle Kingdom does possess many ancient secrets that are not of interest because they are not simplistic or obvious to Westerners. The current repressive government can limit freedoms, but it cannot undo five millennia of history and culture.

It's uncomfortable to view ourselves (Americans) as toddlers in comparison to a wise elder (China, et al), but every inch of discomfort stretches our boundaries and helps us grow.

RUSSIA: MOTHER OF NATIONS

The passport control officer at the Domodedovo airport in Moscow repeatedly barked a word at me that I could not understand. Was he speaking English or Russian? Every Cold War stereotype of a Soviet villain was encapsulated in the tall, black-haired man holding my passport and yelling at me. Dazed and confused, I'd been traveling for over twenty-four hours and was at the end of the immigration line. I felt like I was in a dream with a mean person shouting to wake me up.

"I'm so sorry. I don't understand," I said even though he didn't appear to speak English. I'd learned how to say пожалуйста и спасибо, but please and thank you didn't suffice in this situation. My lack of understanding made him angrier, and he screamed the same word again and again. Finally, a light bulb came on. The word was *Myunkhen*, the Russian pronunciation for Munich.

"Yes, yes, I was on the flight from Munich!" Relief flooded through my exhausted limbs. I smiled a toothy American smile.

The officer rolled his eyes and examined the visa in my passport for longer than seemed necessary. Finally, he stamped my passport as if he were punishing it for my stupidity. He waved me off to baggage claim as if I were a bothersome fly.

As a child and teenager during the Cold War, I learned the Evil Empire was attempting to spread communism throughout the world, most notably in our "backyard" of Central and South America. From antagonists in *Rocky* and *Rambo* to female assassins in James Bond films, Soviet villains were everywhere. Even cartoons depicted nefarious Russian spies. Boris Badenov (a self-proclaimed "nogoodnik") and his comrade and accomplice Natasha Fatale were constantly attempting to steal secret formulas and destroy democracy. Luckily, Rocky and Bullwinkle (a squirrel and a moose) were always able to thwart their evil plans. The passport guy fit the stereotype perfectly.

Americans still perceive Russians as unfriendly and, indeed, Russians don't smile at strangers when passing one in the street.

"Why would we?" my Russian students asked me. "That would be weird."

They perceive the gregariousness of Americans to be superficial and possibly fake. "Americans will smile at you and act friendly but are they going to invite you to their home for dinner?" they pointed out. "No."

"True," I conceded, contemplating all my mostly failed attempts to convince faculty and staff to engage with our international students and scholars.

As a child of the Cold War with an understanding of cultural differences, I wasn't expecting an expansive welcome, but I was dismayed by the blatant unfriendliness of the passport control guy. My mission as a Fulbrighter to increase mutual understanding and support friendly and peaceful relations with people from other countries was off to a rocky start. I had been selected for a Fulbright seminar for community college administrators, an honor beyond my wildest dreams. Much of my professional success came from applying for everything. As I encouraged faculty and colleagues to apply for things, I realized most people aren't willing to spend a lot of time and effort on something without a guarantee of success. They have not because they ask not. Your chances are zero if you don't apply.

Whenever I learned of an opportunity with funding attached, I applied. It required many extra hours of work, but it paid off—not every time, but often enough. Though I had no experience in grant-writing, we obtained numerous capacity building grants to create study abroad programs in France, Guatemala, Ireland, Argentina, and South Africa. These programs were designed to maximize the educational and cultural content for our students, unlike the big tour companies. We were also one of the few community colleges in the country to host Fulbright Foreign Language Teaching Assistants each year: young professionals who came to the States to teach their native languages. Through that program, fully funded by the State Department, we were able to offer Arabic, French, Irish, Portuguese, and Russian language classes in various years to community college students. I adored most of the FLTAs and think of many of them as adopted children along with many of the international students I supervised. Christina, my assistant, bought me a personalized tumbler with "Mother of Nations" printed on it. I'm considering it as the epitaph for my tombstone.

We also hosted Fulbright Scholars-in-Residence—full-fledged professors—from China, Macedonia, and Argentina. Our college quickly became recognized by the State Department for our engagement with Fulbright programs.

The Fulbright program was established in 1946 and is the U.S. government's flagship program for educational and cultural exchange. Every year, thousands of professors and students from the U.S. and abroad participate in short or long-term exchanges to increase mutual understanding through citizen diplomacy. I was grateful for the program in Russia geared specifically to community college administrators; it is hard to compete with university professors for a variety of reasons, including the lack of understanding about community colleges. My travel mates included four other community college administrators—two deans from California and Ohio and two vice presidents from California and Arizona. Over fifteen days we visited various colleges, universities, chambers of commerce, and industries in three Russian cities: Moscow, Perm, and Tyumen. We covered close to 5000 kilometers in those two weeks, not counting getting to and from Moscow. It sounds like a lot until you zoom out and realize we didn't make it halfway across the country.

Once the scary passport guy finally passed me through, I collected my suitcase and made it out of customs, where I found a driver holding a Fulbright sign. His English wasn't great but at least he was friendly. The vice president from Arizona was on the same flight as me and the driver was there to take both of us to the Hotel National, a famous five-star hotel built in 1903 located directly across from the Kremlin. Because the Kremlin had been damaged during the Russian Revolution, the Hotel National had served as the first seat of the Soviet government, with Lenin and his wife residing in room 107 until repairs were made. Enrique, my fellow Fulbrighter from Arizona, and I bonded not only over being Americans, but also over being Spanish-speaking Americans. We talked the driver into stopping at a kiosk where we could exchange some dollars for rubles. The exchange rate was incredible, making me feel like Melinda Gates for the duration of my time in Russia.

After checking into our rooms, I dragged my suitcase along carpeted halls and up and down short flights of stairs until I found my room. The red curtains, bedspread, and chair screamed "Communism," but maybe they were just typical of the era. Heavy wood furniture filled the spacious room, and the large bathroom boasted a walk-in shower. Tempted to flop on the bed, I splashed water on my face and met Enrique in the lobby. When would I ever be in Moscow again? Better take advantage of every opportunity. My excitement for travel was back.

Evening fell as we walked to Red Square, where everything was magically illuminated. At the far end stood St. Basil's

Cathedral, its nine candy-colored onion domes gleaming atop red brick towers. Now a state museum, the iconic structure built by Ivan the Terrible in the 1500s was forcibly secularized in 1924 following the Bolshevik revolution. At the other end of the square stands a small church called Kazan Cathedral. Originally built in the early 1600s, Stalin ordered the church destroyed in 1936. It was the first church rebuilt in the 1990s after the fall of the Soviet Union. I could hear a service going on inside as I bought religious icons from a booth outside for my son Daniel. He had just graduated from college a semester early and was living at home until he started a Master's in Divinity program at Duke in the fall. He had become fascinated by the Orthodox faith and was considering converting.

As I perused the various icons, I couldn't believe the price—a dollar a piece for these cool pieces of religious art. Granted, they were meant for congregants to use in prayer, but they made fantastic souvenirs. Icons were first introduced into the Russian Orthodox faith in the late tenth century. Typically painted on wood, these portraits of saints and depictions of Biblical scenes follow the principles of Byzantine art. Not simply decorative, icons are used for religious devotion (a practice the Reformation would later deem idolatrous). Daniel was especially interested in the most famous of Russian icons: Rublev's Trinity. Also known as The Hospitality of Abraham, this painting depicts the three angels who visited the patriarch in the book of Genesis and are commonly thought by Christians to embody the concept of the triune God: Father, Son, and Holy Spirit.

Hospitality is an important value to me. I've been shown so much of it that I always try to reciprocate. Hosting international students and scholars at Thanksgiving became one of my family's favorite traditions after my parents split. Since the world of our family had cracked, I chose to invite in as many others as I could. I loved having a house crammed full of people who had never experienced Thanksgiving. Having a bunch of surrogate children also eased the pain of my bio kids going off to college and leaving me behind like good American children do.

When Daniel graduated from high school in 2012, I was bereft. I had been melodramatic the entire summer, watching home videocassettes by myself with leaking eyes and bemoaning the end of our family as we knew it. "This is the last time we'll ever eat spaghetti on a Tuesday together as a family again," I would declare.

I insisted on excessive amounts of family time, including our first and only family hike. I got on everyone's damn nerves. Not a surprise that Daniel decided to go to college in Pennsylvania and turn down a full-ride scholarship to my exclusive local alma mater.

"Too close to home," he muttered.

I ended up with a single semester of childfree living when Anna left for college, just enough time to acclimate to not living with ravenous slobs who always took the cash from your wallet. By the time Daniel left for graduate school after his semester back home, Anna was back at home, having decided to do a couple of semesters at the local community college. So my fears were unfounded: My bio kids did not abandon me, and many of my international children keep in touch. I'm now receiving a steady stream of photos of my new "grandbabies" from around the world.

Daniel ultimately chose not to convert to the Orthodox faith and settled on the Episcopal Church, a dramatic shift from his evangelical upbringing. The open displays of the Orthodox faith in Russia surprised me. I assumed that seventy years of the Soviet Union squashing religion succeeded in wiping it out, but I was wrong. Many women wore crosses; many churches had reopened. While Christianity was blossoming again in Russia, they were not particularly welcoming of outside evangelical groups since so many Orthodox priests and faithful adherents had been slaughtered under Communist rule. While Lenin and Stalin lay on one side of Red Square, the sounds of the living faithful emanated from the small church across the cobblestones. I'm sure God was enjoying the irony.

The next morning, I met Linh, the business dean from California. After breakfast, we made our way back to Red Square so we could see Lenin in his mausoleum before departing for Perm. The sun shone on the red granite mausoleum as we waited in line outside the tomb. The doors opened at ten, and the line surged forward. We crept down a few stairs, into a darkened room. I felt unsteady, as if entering a movie theater on a summer day. Lenin's body lay in a glass coffin like Snow White, though hers wasn't bulletproof. Dressed in a nice suit with his beard neatly trimmed, Vladimir's arms rested on a blanket covering his lower torso. The long-dead fingers of his right hand were curled under while the fingers of his left hand stretched out on his body. Lenin, who died in 1924, appeared fresh as a daisy, the result of innovative embalming techniques. The Soviet Union had fallen, but its daddy is still lookin' good.

It's one of the most interesting free things I've seen. Of course, it would be ironic if they charged admission to see the Father of Communism. His suit probably cost a pretty ruble, but he does get a lot of wear out of it. The guards kept the line moving, shuffling us around the coffin and up a short set of stairs into the late spring sunlight. Shielding our eyes with our hands, we circled around the back of the building to see the graves of other notable Russian figures, including Stalin. His embalmed body was originally displayed with Lenin's but later moved out back after knowledge of his genocidal tendencies became widespread.

We saw plenty of statues of Lenin throughout Russia, though many Soviet statues have been removed. Similar debates were occurring in the U.S. at the time about statues representing the Confederacy. This parallel was the first of many notable similarities that surprised me. In North Carolina, students at UNC-Chapel Hill were protesting Silent Sam, the statue of a Confederate soldier that had stood at the entrance of the university for over a century. Primaries for the 2016 election were also underway and I watched in shock and disbelief as a loud-mouthed celebrity millionaire was on his way to becoming the Republican nominee. In Russia, Putin appeared to have equal support. I almost bought my husband a T-shirt of a shirtless Putin riding on the back of a bear. I could see how fear-mongering drives people to crave a "strong man," a leader who will defend them against any perceived enemy. It is easy to hate an enemy when they are "other." When we recognize that we are largely the same, it becomes difficult to justify violence and war. If we think of ourselves as citizen diplomats and strive to promote mutual understanding and peaceful relations, we can indeed make a difference. It's harder to bomb your friends than strangers.

From Moscow, our group flew to Perm, the largest city west of the Ural Mountains, or in other words, the eastern-most city in the European part of Russia. While treated with amazing hospitality everywhere we went, I have to say Perm is one of the ugliest cities I've ever seen. People kept apologizing for the mud everywhere and assuring us it was much nicer in the summer, but frankly that was the least of it. Perm's outdoor artworks include a large bust of Felix Dzerzhinsky, the notorious founder of the KGB, and a sculpture of a dung-beetle made from tires. Need I say more? In contrast to the bleak surroundings, the people welcomed us warmly as we visited the Chamber of Commerce, technical schools, and an aviation college where we met a real live female cosmonaut. Our hosts offered lavish displays of snacks: cabbage and meat rolls, cookies and pastries, circles of bread topped with salmon or slices of meat.

Russian food was hearty with a lot of starchy comfort food. It didn't have European sophistication, but it tasted good. Many Russian women looked less like fashionable Parisians and more like Iowa farm wives. I felt physically comfortable in Russia; my weight was not an anomaly. Obesity was not as prevalent as it is in the U.S., but not everyone was stick skinny. A large lunch lady in white served up generous free meals at one college. She looked like she could fit in perfectly in an American lunchroom. In China the previous year, I had been struck by the vast differences between the East and the West. In Russia, the similarities between our two countries were the surprise. China was an enigma wrapped in a paradox while Russia was a cousin wearing a villain's mask.

From unpretty Perm, we took a day trip to the Kungur Ice Cave, full of visual wonders. As my two male colleagues fought to ride shotgun in the van, I crawled into the back with Andy, the Institute of International Education representative who had created the program in Russia. Andy was an older man with refined Southern manners and a vast knowledge of Russia, having studied in Moscow in the '70s. As we bounced along rough roads, he provided equal amounts of useful information, catty remarks, and witty observations. Giggling with Andy like bad kids in the back of the bus made the pothole bumps worth it.

We struggled out of the van upon arrival at the base of the Ural Mountains on the border between Europe and Asia. Upon entering the cave system, the ceiling reminded me of an old timey icebox in need of defrosting. Lights illuminated the beautiful crystals and icicle stalagmites and stalactites formed hourglass shapes in the grottoes. Peter the Great's geographer discovered fifty grottoes and seventy underground lakes in the 10,000-year-old cave. As we descended the passages, the air temperature grew warmer, a balmy thirty-nine degrees Fahrenheit at the lowest point. The constant changing of temperature and water flow makes the cave a dynamic, living organism.

From there we drove to the White Mountain Monastery, a gleaming white building perched on a snow-covered hill. The gold onion domes glistened on the cloudy day like hope long held in a desolate land. The monastery opened in 1917 and was destroyed a year later by the Bolsheviks who tortured the head monk and threw him in the river below. During the following year, thirty-four monks were tortured and executed by the new communist regime. In 1923 the monastery was closed permanently until it went into use as a facility for invalids under Soviet rule. Finally, in the late 1980s, restoration began on the building. Stark and evocative, I could feel the long years of suffering and disappointment mingled with the tentative feeling of hope. The dark night was over. The Soviet regime had attempted to wipe out religion, but it was blooming again after a long winter of oppression.

We arrived back in Perm in time to pack up and board the Trans-Siberian railway to Tyumen, an oil-rich city and region in Western Siberia. As the train hurtled us through the night, I couldn't sleep thinking about how cool it was to be on the world's longest rail line heading into a land few Americans have visited. It was freaking cool to be somewhere in Siberia in the middle of the night when no one in the world knew exactly where I was. I kept peeking out of the train window but could see nothing until the morning. As day broke, it was snowing lightly as we passed isolated houses scattered miles apart. I watched the barren landscape as I ate the breakfast a porter delivered. My roomie in the sleeper car was the female vice president of a community college in California, a woman about my age with a laconic temperament. We got along fine; she was the least dramatic of our group, and if I snored, she didn't complain about it.

Our hotel in Tyumen was super-fancy, much nicer than the one in Perm. My room was large and decorated all in green, the predominant color for the building. That evening we dined in the hotel restaurant, and it was the best meal for the lowest price I've had in my life. Located on the fourteenth floor, the restaurant was on two levels with a panoramic view of the city. The maître d' showed us to a table by the window covered with a white linen tablecloth. A man in a tuxedo played classical music on a grand piano. I had a gorgeous appetizer of tuna tartare followed by a pasta dish chock full of salmon and caviar. Accompanied by two glasses of a Chilean red, my bill was less than thirty dollars. Russia is full of fascinating delights and it's unfortunate that Putin's regime is making it impossible for Americans to visit. Our Russian hosts and colleagues were delightful and helped me realize the distinction between a government and its people.

In elementary school, my favorite teacher, Miss Stewart, read to my fifth-grade class every day after lunch. Along with *A Wrinkle in Time*, *The Phantom Tollbooth*, and *The Hobbit*, she read us a book about the tsars. Fascinated by the Romanov story, I never forgot Prince Alexei's hemophilia or how his condition was treated by Rasputin, the man who refused to die. From the age of eleven, I was intrigued by Russian history. One of our cultural excursions from Tyumen was to Tobolsk, the historic Siberian capital where Tsar Nicolas II and his family were imprisoned before their murders, except of course for their daughter Anastasia who escaped and perhaps became a Disney princess. (Alas, in 2007, DNA proved that she did not escape and was executed along with the rest of her family.) In addition to the Romanov family, the great writer Fyodor Dostoevsky was also imprisoned there. Another native of Tobolsk is Dmitri Mendeleev, the Russian chemist who designed the periodic table.

In a studio across from the city's stone kremlin, we met an Indigenous orphan-turned-master-craftsman named Minsalim who spent his youth working in a bone-carving factory until the collapse of the Soviet Union. At that point, he started a carving business with his sons, creating detailed figures and scenes from mammoth bones or elk horns, each depicting a myth or legend from the local culture. I chose a carving of a man on skis being pulled by a harnessed reindeer chasing a Siberian husky. Minsalim was quite a character with his wild gray hair, prodigious mustache, and engaging personality. He led my two male colleagues in a shamanic ritual involving handholding, bowing, and many strange chants, grunts, and shouts.

Ignorantly, I had never realized that Russia was full of Indigenous people groups. The Russian tsars massacred and pushed native people off their lands into new territories. Sound familiar? America expanded westward; Russia pushed eastward into Siberia. Similar tactics were used to erase and displace original residents during roughly the same time period. Many Russians compared Siberia to Texas: it was part of Russia but was its own country within a country. A thousand miles from Moscow and on the other side of the Ural Mountains, Siberia did indeed exude a distinct cultural vibe from the Russian capital.

The day after our excursion to Tobolsk, we visited an archeological site which recreated the lifestyles, traditions, and spiritual practices of the Khanty and Mansi people, the Indigenous inhabitants of the area. We were greeted by tall wooden totem poles and then invited into what I would call a teepee. We lay on furs around a small fire and listened to our guide tell us stories. We learned how to cook in a clay oven and how to make spears. We fed a giant billy goat and laughed at the rabbit pen replete with mini teepees. I was struck again by the commonality of peoples: from the Cherokee in North Carolina to the Salish people in the Seattle area to the Māori in New Zealand. All had similar ways of living, the same reliance on stories and spirituality, and the same reverence for the Earth. Perhaps modernity has only separated us from each other.

The delightful day ended in disappointment at a high-end, well-reviewed restaurant in Tyumen which specializes in the cuisine of Northern Siberia. Decorated with indigenous artifacts, the ambiance was intriguing and unique. The menu offered traditional fare such as reindeer hearts, bear stew, and stroganina (thin slices of frozen raw meat.) Appetizing choices were limited for a girl raised on biscuits and country ham. I don't remember what I ordered because I never received it. We were all famished enough to eat a bear, but the restaurant was incredibly slow. After two hours of waiting for our food, we stomped out like the Americans we were and headed to the McDonald's next to our hotel. I'm not sure if Olga, our Fulbright coordinator, was more embarrassed for us or by us.

I've hardly mentioned the meetings and campus tours that comprised most of our itinerary. I've not elaborated on the strong personalities and constant closeness which forced our little group into a dysfunctional family. I've barely spoken about our last days back in Moscow, from our stay in the Hotel Metropol (setting for Amor Towles' *A Gentleman in Moscow*) to our debriefing and lunch at the U.S. Embassy, to our tour of the beautiful artwork in the subway stations. I didn't even talk about the Krispy Kreme store, a company based in my hometown, that I found on a side street off Red Square, glowing like a mirage from home.

Throughout my Fulbright experience, I was struck by how similar Russians are to Americans. There are so many commonalities. Both countries are geographically large and linguistically isolated. Both countries expanded their territory by displacing Indigenous populations. Even Texas and Siberia have commonalities. The Christian faith is embedded in the fiber of both nations. We both fought the Nazis in World War II and feared each other during the Cold War.

I had assumed Russians were our opposites, but I discovered they were our mirror image.

Recently, the Russian government named the Institute of International Education (IIE), the nonprofit that administers the Fulbright program, as an "undesirable organization." Under Russian law, undesirable organizations are forbidden from all activity and operations in the country, and anyone affiliated with them could be subject to fines or imprisonment of up to six years. I'm so glad I was able to witness firsthand the country that mesmerized me in childhood and created fear in my youth. Meeting kind and gracious people showed me the real Russia. Citizen diplomacy is the key to peace. To paraphrase the cartoon *Pogo*, "I have met the enemy, and they are us." We can never see ourselves; it's only our reflection that shows us who we are.

To this day, I struggle with the black and white thinking of my childhood. We're all raised to think of ourselves as the good guys and someone else as the enemy. My experience in Russia brought home the truth that no one sees himself as the bad guy. We all justify our actions. Since no one has the full picture except God, maybe we really should leave the judging to Him.

CUBA: CONFESSIONS OF A LESSER CAPITALIST

My appendix ruptured on the way home from Cuba. A couple of the men in our Community Travel Club group were feeling poorly, so I assumed I'd been stricken with the same avenging travel virus. Sitting on the toilet in the Miami airport, I clutched my stomach, waiting for diarrhea that never came. By midnight in the van back to campus from the Charlotte airport, I was delirious. When Craig finally pulled our car into our driveway, I dragged myself upstairs to our bedroom, leaving my suitcase and backpack in the car. The next day, I couldn't get out of bed.

"I could be dead for all you care," I muttered when Craig finally peeked into the bedroom toward nightfall. At that point I was just trying to make him feel bad; I didn't realize it was true.

On Sunday, I was still bed-ridden, nauseated and feverish, debating on whether I should see a doctor before going to work on Monday. Missing work was not something I did. How could the Universe turn without me? Concerned that I might have a deadly and communicable tropical virus, I made an appointment. The doctor listened as I described the pain in the lower right-quadrant of my abdomen, a red rash, and a low-grade fever.

"Strep throat," she diagnosed, prescribing amoxicillin.

The antibiotic helped a bit, so I went back to work. A week later at a U2 concert in Philadelphia, as I tried to enjoy the show with over 56,000 other fans, I thought *Damn-I'm-too-old-for-this* because I couldn't stand for the entire show. I had to sit down between every few songs. Anna and her boyfriend Kameron had gone with us to U2's 30th anniversary tour of *The Joshua Tree* at Lincoln Financial Field. Their tickets were on the field, while we had seats in the stands. As bacteria leaked into an abscess in my abdomen, Anna was suffering from anxiety and dehydration. She spent most of the show in the first aid tent and even vomited on poor Kameron's shoe, but he was gallant and sweet and didn't mind missing most of the concert. She talked us into leaving before the end of the encore, which I have never done. Leaving a U2 show early? Another clue that something was seriously wrong with me. As we rode the train back to our car, I contemplated the lack of spiritual ecstasy from this show. Highly unusual.

Back in North Carolina, I finished my prescription of antibiotics and started to feel worse. I begrudgingly made another appointment with the doctor at Craig's insistence. My regular doctor was out of the office, but I was happy enough to see the incredibly dreamy physician's assistant. I used to be dismissive of PAs, but this one saved my life when the real doctor almost killed me.

"Um, you need a CT scan, like now," the handsome PA told me nervously. "It's almost five o'clock, but I'll see if they'll stay open for you."

I swung by the house to pick up Craig and sped across town to the imaging center. After a few dunks of my body into a metal tube, the anonymous, omniscient readers of the scan sent a message advising me to go straight to the ER. They didn't talk to us in person nor tell us why we needed to go to the ER, but we obeyed. Approximately fifty-seven hours after checking into the hospital, someone pulled back the curtain surrounding the not comfy bed and informed me that my appendix had burst two-and-a-half weeks ago.

"Holy crap, doesn't that mean you should be dead?" Everyone who hears this story asks the same question.

"Ha, ha, it's not as fatal as we've all been led to believe!" I laugh nonchalantly and reply gaily.

"Maybe you're just too mean to die," Craig mutters.

My cousin Lee says I'm a badass for hiking a mile through parking lots, dumpsters, and ravines with a ruptured appendix to drink a beer out of the back of his pickup before the U2 show with him and his lovely wife, Meredith. Lee is my favorite New Jersey cousin, the only one I really keep in touch with. It was cool that he drove to the concert to see us and listen to the show from the parking lot. And I like that he called me a badass when he found out my situation.

Sure, I'm a fat, middle-aged woman with a bum knee, but on the inside, I'm as hard as a calculus exam. I love thinking of myself as a tough old broad. I pride myself on my stoic capacity for enduring pain without flinching. Perhaps a high tolerance for pain shouldn't be a point of pride, but I can't see myself moaning or wailing under any circumstance. I love it when medical staff tell me I'm a good (i.e. not difficult) patient. My childhood good girl eats that shit up.

After my "strep throat" was re-diagnosed as a leaky appendix, I spent three nights in the hospital being pumped full of massive amounts of IV antibiotics. The doctors didn't remove my appendix at this point; surgery wasn't advisable with all those bacteria swirling around my innards. I did shed a few silent tears when sweet Nurse Rebecca repeatedly stabbed my hand veins in the middle of the night trying unsuccessfully to start a second IV. She then pumped potassium through the new IV which is surely some torture tactic invented by ISIS. But I didn't groan or scream. I just allowed a few more quiet tears to run down my cheek. When the residents came around on the day I was being released, they were amazed to see I hadn't been taking any pain meds. Hell, I walked around with a ruptured appendix for over two weeks. Why would I need pain meds now that I was being treated?

It's interesting to think about what would have happened had my appendix ruptured in Cuba a day earlier. Cuban communism has its upsides, and excellent medicine is one of them. Of course, they have crappy equipment and facilities because of the decades of economic embargo. Who knows how my treatment would have gone there but it would have been free.

"Aren't you so glad you made it home before this happened?" people ask.

"Yes," I reply. *Maybe,* I think.

It's possible I would have been diagnosed correctly right away and treated with zero out-of-pocket expense, but I don't know that for sure. Life expectancy is higher in Cuba than in the U.S. and infant mortality is lower. In addition to excellent medical care, other highly touted benefits of Cuban communism include a 99.8 percent literacy rate and free, quality higher education. Just imagine: no medical bills and no saving for the kids to go to college. Some aspects of socialism seem downright fabulous.

However, there's the other side of the story: the anti-American rhetoric, the alliances with our enemies, the repression of basic freedoms, and the widespread human rights violations. At the Bay of Pigs memorial, I read the signs in Spanish which describe Americans as "cowardly imperialist mercenaries who murdered innocent women and children, hiding behind the ridiculous notion of God." I was glad no one in our group could read Spanish. Even though I understand how propaganda works and try not to be goaded by insults, it raised my hackles.

Depictions of Ché and Fidel are ubiquitous throughout Cuba, almost always accompanied by the slogan *Hasta la Victoria Siempre* (Ever Onward to Victory.) A sign outside the airport showed a Cuban fist punching Uncle Sam in the nose. Another billboard depicted the U.S. as a greedy consumerist monster gobbling up the world. In Havana, we passed a mural depicting a sharp-toothed humanoid perching atop a black mass labeled "the 99 percent." Names of western companies were scribbled all over his hideous body.

Yet, without fail, every single person we met was kind and friendly to us. No one held the embargo against us or seemed to perceive us as greedy, cowardly, murderous mercenaries. Several people told us they prefer Americans to Europeans because we're friendly and we tip. Yay us!

As we talked with musicians and artists and children and seniors, we discovered a real sense of community among the Cuban people. I was surprised to learn that most of them seemed to believe in the goals of *la Revolución*. They were proud of what they had accomplished despite the decades of sanctions: achievements in medicine and literacy and the arts. They were staunch in their dedication to helping each other. For example, giving rides to anyone who needs one is ingrained in the culture. You just stand by the side of the road and whoever comes along picks you up. We were clearly meeting people the Cuban government wanted us to meet, but they appeared to be sincere in their support of the regime.

There is widespread poverty in Cuba, but it was a different kind of poverty from what I'd seen elsewhere. It took a while for me to notice what I wasn't seeing: homeless people, street kids, malnourished children, corrugated tin shacks, trash, crime, billboards advertising products people can't afford to buy, rich people to envy. Yes, they all had crappy little houses, but *they all* had crappy little houses. I went to Cuba "glad to see it before it changes," but I left thinking they may not succumb to consumerism as quickly as we think they will. Money is a powerful temptation, but a firm belief in equity may stand up against greed. Since the U.S. policy toward Cuba changed again shortly after our return, it's moot at this point. Our Community Travel Club tour was an educational people-to-people exchange, one of a handful of legal ways Americans could visit Cuba at the time. The Trump administration subsequently did away with this visa category, so we really did go at the right time.

When we first landed in Cienfuegos, a French colonial city in the middle of the island on the south side, we taxied to the end of the runway, turned around and parked in front of a small square building. You can do that when you're the only plane at the airport. Deplaning onto the hot tarmac, we were greeted by a slew of airport employees. There was about a one-to-one ratio of employees to passengers. The most curious sight was all the young women in their official looking uniforms that included miniskirts and black lace stockings. I felt like I'd landed in a distant galaxy in an early Star Trek episode. The terminal consisted of one room with a couple of old-timey conveyor belts that slowly delivered our luggage. The vast sea of airport employees helped us go through customs and passport control. They were thorough (earned their government pay), but friendly.

As soon as we walked to our bus, we started to see all the vintage cars. In the 1950s, when Cuba was the playground of the rich and famous, celebrities and mobsters filled Havana's streets with Chevys, Fords, Buicks, Pontiacs, and Studebakers. In the decades since, Cubans have found ingenious ways to keep these cars running. A misconception is that these are the only cars in Cuba. Cubans imported automobiles from the Soviet Union and Eastern Europe throughout the Castro regimes. It was only when tourists started going crazy over them, that Cubans began painting the American Classics in bright colors and restoring them to mint condition. Still, they do create an ambiance of having traveled back in time. Havana itself looks like the set of a post-Apocalyptic thriller. The beauty of the crumbling city is apparent, yet much is in decay. A few buildings have been restored and painted, but outside the main tourist areas, the overall image is of a city forgotten by time.

We were greeted at our first hotel with trays of mojitos, which we drank daily. Everywhere we went, waiters would hand us a glass of fresh-squeezed tropical juice in a glass filled an inch or two short of the top. Another waiter would subsequently come around offering to fill the glass with rum. Everyone in our group graciously accepted the top off whenever it was offered. We had a most excellent group. The best mojitos were at the Hotel Nacional pool bar, the thick grains of sugar settling among the mint leaves at the bottom of the plastic cups, an extra treat to suck through the straw when you reached the end of the drink.

The Hotel Nacional is Havana's iconic hotel where the rich and famous used to play. Palm trees line the road leading to the gleaming white hotel which is perched on a hill near the sea. Inside, gleaming tiles, Spanish arches, and wood-beamed ceilings take you back in time. Constructed in 1930, it hosted guests from Frank Sinatra to Winston Churchill to Jean-Paul Sartre to Jimmy Carter. In 1946, the "Havana Conference" took place in the hotel's casino—a meeting between the American and Sicilian Mafia, a scene which was recreated in *The Godfather 2*, though filmed in the Dominican Republic. Truly a five-star hotel in its day, the nightly rate was around $139 a night when we were there.

Much of our program involved meeting local musicians and artists and craftsmen. Music was everywhere: from the traditional Afro-Cuban *son* played by a band at our outdoor dinner, to a baroque trio with an amazingly talented teenaged boy on violin, to a classical string ensemble playing Spanish Renaissance music in an eighteenth-century mansion. Walking the streets of Old Havana, a woman in traditional dress belted out *El Manisero* (The Peanut Vendor) as she offered to sell us paper cones of roasted peanuts for a few pennies. We visited a senior citizen club called *Alegría de Vivir* (Joy of Living) where they taught us to play a game with a wooden stick and a piece of rubber and later how to dance rumba. Their *alegría de vivir* was apparent and clearly not manufactured for tourists. It was the same with art: Everywhere we went, we encountered sculptors and painters and craftsmen and muralists. One neighborhood in the outskirts of Havana called *Muraleando* is entirely dedicated to art and music, the streets full of murals and artwork for blocks. It's a magical place.

On our last night in Havana, we had dinner at a *paladar* (a privately owned restaurant) called *La Moraleja*. The name struck me as a curious choice: The Moral. It was pouring rain, and we had to brave a flash flood to enter. Waiters armed with umbrellas whisked us from the bus across the surging waters into the safety of the restaurant. Once inside, our group had the place to ourselves while an award-winning jazz trio played unobtrusively at the end of the room. Plate after plate was set before us. Glass after glass was filled. Within the oasis of La Moraleja we chattered contentedly, sheltered in a peaceful oasis in a once beautiful city. After dinner, the wait staff arrived with a shot of rum and a cigar on the house for each of us. Though I posed with it, I didn't smoke my cigar. Craig grabbed it and secreted it into his growing stash to carry home. He maxed out his quota on *cubanos* and Havana Club rum.

As often happens when enjoying wonderful meals in elegant restaurants, my mind wandered back to my own waitressing days in high school and college. The restaurant where I had worked was more of a bar and the cast of characters who worked and drank there resembled a Greek comedy, a Mexican telenovela, an American reality TV show. Our regulars had included a Moroccan hairdresser who claimed to have cut the Beatles' hair, an assertion supported by the photo of him grinning with the Fab Four. One of our least favorite customers was a semi-famous, one-armed artist who had painted the Queen of England's portrait. There was a very handsome-yet-annoying surgeon who always came in wearing short-shorts and carrying a can of Diet Coke. We were shocked when he had gender reassignment surgery; that was not a common occurrence in the '80s.

We referred to ourselves as *waitrons*, scurrying around, slinging drinks and delivering food while our cigarette burned down in a glass ashtray in the kitchen. Often a secret shot gifted from the bartender appeared on a shelf in the pantry, waiting for us to have a moment to down it. I thought of the time my friend Shannon and I "went for the gold" during the summer Olympics of 1986, using straws to suck down eight tall Russian Quaaludes (vodka, Bailey's, Kahlua) together during our shift. We made so much money that night. Drunk waitressing made us extra amiable, I suppose.

Sitting in the restaurant in Havana, it seemed unreal that Shannon had died over a year before. She caught a cold which became pneumonia which became leukemia which became death, possibly due to a botched procedure. She had gone from a vibrant and healthy woman in her early fifties to dead in a matter of days. She was my first real friend to pass away. Though we didn't see each other constantly, our friendship had lasted beyond our waitressing days. Our children were born around the same time, and they played together while Shannon and I watched *The Lord of the Rings* on DVD a zillion times. The kids trick-or-treated together and attended each other's birthday parties. As our children grew older, Shannon and I met for a coffee a couple of times a year to catch up. I still couldn't believe she was gone.

Weeks later as they wheeled me through the labyrinth of hospital corridors to drain the abscess created by my ruptured appendix, my mind drifted to Shannon. Lying on the gurney, I stared at the ceiling as a random person pushed me for what seemed like miles. I had visited Shannon in the hospital and couldn't shake how unlike herself she looked, bloated and unconscious. I talked to her and prayed for her.

Her death is still incomprehensible to me. Why had she died while I had walked around with a leaky appendix for weeks and lived? What was the moral of that story? Why do some live and others die? Lying alone in the hospital made me pensive. Even though I thought death was finished making a run at me, it had just stopped to catch its breath.

The dinner at La Moraleja had me pondering a lot of morals. In addition to contemplating Shannon's senseless death, I thought about the moral of the Cuban story. I hadn't really planned a tour of communist countries; my back-to-back visits to China, Russia, and Cuba were coincidental, even though I assumed I was probably now on some government list due to my choices of destination. Warm climate communism was so different from the frigid shards of Soviet communism I witnessed in Russia or the reserved, high-context communism in China.

While the Soviet Union was long gone, la Revolución marched on ninety miles off the U.S. coast on an island full of humidity, art, rum, music, tobacco and advanced medicine. It was definitely a more festive version of communism. Cubans still seemed to believe in Castro's ideals. And yet, they also seem to genuinely like Americans despite history and propaganda and economics. Maybe the mere fact that humans have ideals is enough of a unifying factor. Even if we don't agree on any specifics, we all believe things should be better. We all want to earn a living, love our families, and live in peace.

Even Shannon and I didn't share all the same ideals, but we genuinely cared for each other. There's always common ground if you're willing to look for it.

ARGENTINA: WHAT THE HEART WHISPERS

It's Sunday morning in Villa María, a city of 80,000 smack dab in the center of Argentina. The sun is streaming in through the glass doors of the common room in the Babel Buen Hostel, though the June air is chilly. It's winter here, south of the equator. It's quiet now—my students are sound asleep after spending all night at the club. Despite the chilly weather, the lemon tree in the courtyard overlooking the small, drained swimming pool is full of ripe fruit. Marcos, the owner of the hostel, had picked lemons from the tree and made fresh squeezed lemonade for us, insisting, "*Sí, sí, tiene azúcar,*" although we all found it supremely sour.

Marcos is a tall man of maybe sixty who has ridden his motorcycle around South America, adores his grandchildren, and opened the hostel a couple of years ago to fulfill a lifelong dream. Each morning, he serves us croissants (called *medialunas* in Argentina), *bizcochos* (a square, hard biscuit), and *café con leche*. There is a fresh inspirational quote written on the blackboard in Marcos' hand which he asks me to translate daily for my students. Two nights ago, he prepared an authentic Argentine *asado* for us, showing us how to light the fire, salt the meat, and grill the various cuts of beef and pork. We ate at a long wobbly table, Argentines and Americans, young and old.

Two days before the *asado*, we visited a soup kitchen for children, where hungry kids come for milk and bread. Many of them were Bolivian immigrants and we learned about the cultural differences between Argentina and Bolivia, along with a few words of Quechua. We put together Oriental Trading crafts of owls holding American flags, owls being the symbol of Villa María. Grant, my super-tall student, enjoyed lifting the children high in the air, much to their delight. In the back room, was a clothing closet with a faded picture of Jesus watching over the piles of shoes and pants and blouses. A lump formed in my throat and my eyes threatened to leak. It was a beautiful thing: students from NC community colleges singing, dancing, and playing with Argentine and Bolivian children, all having fun. I was humbled that I had a hand in this unlikely and joyous encounter. I'd written and received a grant to create the study abroad program in Argentina which included a partnership with two other local community colleges. I was spreading the international education gospel beyond my own institution, building capacity for study abroad for community college students across the state of North Carolina.

Strangely enough, it was around this time that the word *legend* began appearing in connection with my name. A couple of months prior to the Argentina program, I had received the Werner Kubsch award for lifetime achievement in international education from CCID (Community Colleges for International Development). I had to give an acceptance speech at the annual conference from a stage in a ballroom.

From the moment I learned I would receive the award, my heart filled with dread. The thought of standing on that stage speaking to hundreds of people terrified me. Adding to the terror was my belief that my speech had to be *great*. Though we had achieved impressive results at my college for an institution of our size, I still felt like a bumbling amateur compared to many of my sophisticated colleagues who knew how to dress impeccably, speak discretely and diplomatically, and throw out terms like *value proposition* and *operationalize* without rolling their eyes. Not to mention that I was fat, which clearly meant I was unworthy. I felt overwhelming pressure to prove that I deserved the award I had been awarded.

By this point in my life, teaching and presenting were so familiar to me that I spent little time planning my lessons or presentations. But anxiety about the speech spurred me to prepare like my children's lives depended on it. I wrote the speech, recorded the speech, listened to the speech, memorized the speech, and practiced it over and over. I have never prepared for anything more. The speech needed a balance of gratitude and humility, funny anecdotes, and a thought-provoking message. It couldn't be too long. For my theme I chose "the banality of the miraculous," in contrast to Hannah Arendt's concept of the banality of evil. Knees shaking but voice steady, I spoke of watching rural Christian students show up at the airport to hug and cry and snap selfies with North African Muslim students who were returning home after a year in North Carolina. I talked about standing with community college students in the Sistine Chapel, on the Great Wall of China, at the lip of a volcano in Costa Rica, in front of the ruins of the crematoria at Auschwitz. I thanked my president for her support and joked about how I secretly gloated over my colleagues' president envy. I concluded by thanking all my colleagues for being miracle workers. Basically, I killed it. I *crushed* it. I could feel months' worth of built-up anxiety drain from my body as I left the stage, only vaguely aware of the standing ovation. Thus, my status as legend was cemented.

I didn't feel like a legend in Argentina. God never lets me get too carried away with myself. Getting the program together seemed cursed. In addition to all the work involved in getting the UNVM partnership off the ground, it was a nightmare getting students to sign up, pay their money, attend the class, and apply for their passports. Student after student dropped out, neglected to pay on time, and didn't complete their homework. The politest student who turned in all his forms and assignments on time was committed to a mental hospital and advised not to travel by his doctor. Of the six students who managed to make it to Argentina, four of them were problematic in one way or another.

But on this sunny Sunday morning while my students were sleeping as I sipped *café con leche*, life was good. The night before, we had gone to Mass in the Cathedral. I found my eyes leaking there, too, touched by the beauty of the candles illuminating the golden altar, the priest's green vestments and the unique paintings and statues. A choir accompanied by guitar softly led the singing. The sight of older men kneeling in reverence to God on the hard floor pierced my heart. Though my Protestant disdain for excess is still a part of me, I've learned to appreciate the beauty of a sacred space, a true sanctuary from the outside world.

It was nice to have a little downtime after an extremely busy week. Our Argentine hosts kept us going from morning until evening. We spent our weekdays in class at the university from early in the morning until late in the afternoon. Sometimes we had an activity in the evening—a tango lesson or an exhibition of other folkloric dances. We usually ate dinner at the Bar Argentino or the empanada shop down the block, the only restaurants that opened by 8 p.m., our American stomachs unable to adjust to the cultural difference in dinnertime. We learned that we had to ask for the bill. At first, we thought it rude that we sat at the table so long after finishing and the waiters didn't bring the check.

"They must be ignoring us because we're Americans," one of my students suggested.

"Maybe, maybe not," I cautioned, though I too was a little miffed about the poor service.

Upon discussing it with our colleagues, we learned that in Argentina a waiter would never bring the bill if not requested; it would be considered rude to rush people. I think of this now at home whenever a server slaps down the check along with my dinner plate.

In the U.S., time is money. In Argentina, time is for people.

The Universidad Nacional de Villa María is a young university and has a lot in common with U.S. community colleges. A trio of female professors arranged our itinerary, leading us from class to class and from activity to activity. All three were tiny and energetic, clothed in tight pants and heeled boots. My large body did not fit in in this country, which ranks second in the world in cases of anorexia (Japan has the highest number.) I couldn't understand it—Argentina is full of amazing food: beef, red wine, empanadas, and *milanesas* (breaded cutlets). My favorite treat was *alfajores*—the iconic Argentine shortbread cookies sandwiched with *dulce de leche* in the middle. Here is a conversation I have heard verbatim dozens of times:

American trying dulce de leche for the first time: "Oh, it's like caramel!"

Argentine extremely insulted by the comparison: "It is *not* like caramel. It's milk jam."

American reconsidering eating the cookie: "Ew, that sounds terrible."

I'm not sure why Argentines are so outraged by the simile, but it is so predictable I get a kick out of it. Even if *dulce de leche* is prepared similarly to jam—milk and sugar heated together—it's hard to explain why "milk jam" sounds disgusting to American ears.

Our days started with a P.E. class (Zumba) taught by the mayor's wife—a pretty but extremely thin woman. The Americans followed her lead, dancing enthusiastically if awkwardly alongside the Argentine students. We had met the mayor on our site visit in March and he is an attractive man. My colleagues kid me about having a crush on him, but I think I just say out loud what everyone else is thinking. A couple of years after the first program, the mayor left his skinny wife for a man. Shocking that being thin isn't a guarantee of a perfect life.

On Thursday night we had our own private tango lesson at a studio in town, with a handsome instructor and his pregnant wife. Argentines are also almost entirely of European ancestry, and many are blond and light-eyed. I knew Argentina was "the most European" country in South America, but it wasn't until I went there that I learned that virtually everyone in Argentina *is* European. Like the U.S., they're a nation of immigrants. Their ancestors came largely from Spain, Italy, and Germany. There wasn't a large Indigenous population when the Europeans arrived in the Land of Silver. Argentines eat pasta and croissants and drink Fernet (a disgusting Italian liqueur which tastes like herbal cough medicine) with Coke. They have a reputation among other South Americans as being snobs. The only non-European thing about them is that they eat their famous beef well-done, a great tragedy.

Argentines also love dogs more than any people I've ever seen. The streets of Villa María are full of strays, and everyone treats them kindly. The dogs are everywhere, including the university cafeteria where we had lunch every day. I have a great picture of my student Melissa's face when a tall dog sidled up to her and began eating directly off her tray. When we got to Buenos Aires there were dog-walkers everywhere, especially in the neighborhood near the U.S. Embassy. A dozen or so dogs of varying breeds and sizes trotted happily along the wide sidewalks attached to leashes leading to the walker's hand. Grant, our super tall student, was terrified of all the dogs including the teeny tiny ones. Maybe I shouldn't have laughed, but I found it comical to see this massive man-child startle and hide behind me at the sight of an itsy-bitsy canine.

Grant was like a toddler in a giant's body. I recruited him for the trip because he seemed thoughtful and responsible. Which just goes to show you don't really know anyone until you travel out of the country with them. He was chronically late, including holding up the group by thirty minutes on our way to the airport. He could not understand why I was so upset since we didn't miss our flight. During our Spanish lessons at UNVM, he refused to pay attention. He swiped through Tinder in full view of everyone. He drank to excess. Worst of all, he had boundary issues: Once he laid his head in my lap as we were sitting on a sofa in the hotel lobby. Another time I found him lying on my bed in the hostel. I don't think it was sexual; I believe he thought of me as a mother. Even though he drove me crazy with his inappropriate behavior, I was still fond of him. I spoke to him repeatedly about the rules for the study abroad program, but I couldn't get him to comply. I warned him that he could be sent home, but he didn't believe I would do it.

Mikayla, on the other hand, was an ideal student. A young wife and mother, she was polite, paid attention, and seemed to enjoy everything. She was an especially good dancer, mastering both the tango and the folkloric dances we learned. She was a model study abroad participant. Until she wasn't. On our last day in Villa María, our hosts were planning to take us to the Estancia Yucat, a working ranch owned by the Catholic Church. I was excited that we weren't leaving until eleven; we had gotten up early every other day. By ten-thirty, I had seen everyone except for Mikayla. Even Grant was awake and ready to go. When I quizzed Mikayla's roommates, they hemmed and hawed, eyeing the floor. After piercing them with my teacher-mother death gaze, they confessed that she was with Fabio. This is one name I have not changed because sometimes truth is stranger than fiction. When your married mother student runs off with a man in South America, who else could it be but Fabio?

Mikayla had met Fabio the previous weekend at the club. After we returned from a Rotary Club party, she snuck out and Fabio picked her up. I reviewed the hostel's security tape as if I were a CSI detective. Mikayla wasn't answering her phone nor responding to anything we sent through Messenger. When the university representatives arrived to take us to the ranch, they were horrified and scandalized by the situation. I was concerned about Mikayla but also embarrassed by her behavior. The university's head international officer insisted I go to the police station and file a missing person's report. A staff member I didn't know accompanied me to the station, just a few blocks away from our hostel. A police officer was questioning me when we got a call saying Mikayla had responded to the messages and was headed back to the hostel. Equal parts of relief and anger flooded through me. Now that I knew she was safe, I was super annoyed.

The rest of the group headed on to the ranch, while I waited for Mikayla to return to the hostel. I didn't relish the thought of having to deal with the situation. She'd been such an ideal participant except for this incident. What the heck was I going to say to her? I thought about Marcos' hand-written quote on the blackboard that morning:

Es imposible, dice el orgullo.
Es arriesgado, dice la experiencia.
No tiene sentido, dice la razón.
Inténtalo, susurra el corazón.

It's impossible, says Pride.
It's risky, says Experience.
It doesn't make sense, says Reason.
Try it, whispers the heart.

Mikayla and I went to a restaurant down the block for lunch. She seemed contrite and understood how serious the situation was. I didn't talk to her about morality or her personal life, but I did reiterate the rules of the study abroad program and the importance of representing our college and our country well. She told me a little about her marriage and kids and her husband's depression and lack of work. It's not hard to understand the allure of running away from a mundane and difficult life into the arms of a Latin lover. What else explains the success of *the* Fabio? I am the queen of escape fantasies, but I'm convinced I would never cross the fantasy-reality line.

Of course, I thought my father would never cross it either.

Feeling pretty good about how I'd handled the Mikayla situation, I spent the rest of the afternoon packing. The following day we left Villa María and traveled ninety minutes to Córdoba, Argentina's second largest city. After a tour of the City Square, the Jesuit Block, and the Cathedral, we had the rest of the day free. Scott, an Early College math instructor who was a paying participant on the trip, and Grant and I sat in a bar across from the hotel and watched Croatia devastate Argentina three-zip in the World Cup. The home crowd slowly lost hope: sadness and disgust replacing team pride goal by goal. I don't think it was schadenfreude; I wasn't taking pleasure in their pain, but I was detached from their misery. Humans can take games awfully seriously.

I imposed an 11 p.m. curfew for our night in Córdoba. We were in a big city and needed to leave for the airport to head for Buenos Aires at 5 a.m. I dragged my suitcase out of the elevator into the lobby at 4:55 a.m. and was happy to see several people were already downstairs. The bus was outside waiting for us. Of course, Grant wasn't down yet, and I didn't see Mikayla. Shortly after 5 a.m., the two entered the lobby together from the street. Ignoring the curfew, they had been out at a club all night. With

Fabio, who had followed us from Villa María. *Fue la gota que colmó el vaso*, the drop that filled the glass. They weren't even packed.

I informed them to get their bags on the bus and that instead of going to Buenos Aires with us, they would both be going home.

I contemplated calling my boss, but it was 4 a.m. at home. I waited until we arrived at the airport and found out I would need to rebook them out of Buenos Aires anyway. Once we arrived in BA, I confirmed with my boss and the president that I should indeed send them home, and to use my personal credit card, since both were claiming they didn't have three hundred dollars for the rebooking fee. Scott took the rest of the group to the hotel, while I spent an hour on the phone changing their flights. I gave them their flight information, let them know that their plane was leaving late that evening from the city's other major airport, and walked out the door (also approved by my supervisors.)

As soon as she got home, Mikayla sent me an apologetic email. She really was sorry, and I had empathy for her situation. She had confessed to her husband immediately and was working through it. Grant, on the other hand, was upset with me for a long time, but we eventually made peace. For the life of me, I can't figure out why they didn't just come back fifteen minutes earlier. If they'd slipped into the lobby at 4:45 a.m. and brought their bags down, I never would have known. If you're going to break the rules, at least be smart about it. If you're going to follow your heart, don't leave your brain out of it completely.

I didn't have any doubts that I had done the right thing. They'd both been given verbal warnings and second chances (or about fifty chances in Grant's case). However, I did feel a little bad for them to miss the last couple of days in the capital city. On the other hand, I felt much lighter and freer.

The rest of the group spent our drama-free time posing in the Olympic rings in front of the iconic *obelisco*, which looks just like a small version of the Washington monument. The rings were there for the 2018 Youth Olympics and would later be hoisted into the air for the opening ceremony. We strolled down the *Avenida 9 de Julio*, the world's widest street with fourteen lanes. In the Recoleta cemetery, a veritable city of the dead, we wandered among elaborate above-ground marble mausoleums. Posing next to the tomb of Eva Perón, I hummed *Don't cry for me, Argentina*. Our smaller group posed in front of *la Casa Rosada*, i.e., the President's workplace. In the *La Boca* neighborhood, birthplace of the tango, we enjoyed the colorful buildings, artistic offerings, and dancers performing at outdoor cafés. *La Bombonera* stadium, home to the Boca Juniors soccer team, is another attraction of the barrio. Diego "the hand of God" Maradona played here. Maradona wasn't a great human being, but he led Argentina to the World Cup championship in 1986 and is revered as a cultural icon. Yep, me and Maradona, both legends.

Our group agreed to spend our last full day taking a ferry to Uruguay to see the city of Colonia. Delighted to check off another country, we roamed the stone streets of the historic quarter visiting vine-covered shops and charming cafés. The following day, our flight home left Buenos Aires at midnight. We checked out of the hotel in the morning and spent another day running around the city. Exhausted, we arrived at the airport late in the evening and boarded our 11-hour flight to New York. Nothing annoys me more than flying two hours past our destination, but we didn't have a choice. To make matters worse, we had a nine-hour layover in JFK before our connection back to Charlotte.

On the way to Argentina, I had taken the group into the city for a quick walk around Times Square and a slice of pizza. None of us was inclined to move a muscle on the return even though we had the time. We slumped in plastic chairs as the minutes and hours ticked by until finally it was time to board. Realizing we hadn't seen Talia in a while, I frantically began to look for her. I knew her phone was not working. Finally, my students convinced me to board without her. She was in her mid-thirties, and they figured she could make it home from New York on her own. As it turned out, she had managed to get rebooked on an earlier flight but didn't bother to tell me. Sigh.

Argentina evokes mixed feelings for me—the student issues were dismaying, but I believe that each of them benefited from the experience. In *El Aleph*, a short story by Jorge Luis Borges, Argentina's most famous author, the protagonist visits the cellar of his dead wife's cousin. There he witnesses the Aleph—a small iridescent orb which contains all the points of the universe simultaneously visible without overlapping.

When I think about Argentina, my mind simultaneously sees history combined with memory, a blend of facts and personal experience. Gauchos galloping on the pampas. My meek student Colton excelling at tango due to his marching band background. People being disappeared during the Dirty War. Mothers marching at the Plaza de Mayo. An old man kneeling on the marble of the cathedral. Messi scoring a goal. Grant lifting a child high in the air at the soup kitchen. Evita giving a speech from a balcony. Drinking malbec with my colleagues. Pope Francis bartending in his youth. A dog eating from Melissa's tray in the university cafeteria. Employees serving up empanadas at the shop around the corner. Argentines fighting to take back the Falkland islands. American students sipping *mate* from the thermoses of Argentine students. Marcos writing quotes on the chalkboard in the breakfast room of the hostel.

Marcos may not be Borges, but his quotes inspired me all the same.

Somos el resultado de los libros que leemos
Los cafés que disfrutamos,
Los viajes que hacemos,
Y las personas que amamos.

We are the product of the books we read,
the cups of coffee we enjoy,
the trips we take,
and the people we love.

Books, coffee, travel, and loved ones. These are the things that make me whole. I may be a legend now, but I'm still a chubby nerd who loves to read and explore the world with students, friends, and family. Each of my journeys contains a universe, each is a volume of history and experience I can dust off and examine at will. The characters spring back to life and I can smell and taste and hear the essence of the place. My metaphorical bookcase is full of a hundred true stories. I am a lucky woman. I've lived an unexpected life.

IRELAND: TREAD SOFTLY
ON MY DREAMS

My cat alerted me to the arrival of the Jehovah's Witnesses. Finn is an evil genius, and I adore him. One of his best qualities is that, unlike my sweet dumb dog, he is mostly silent. Occasionally he'll meow for breakfast or dinner, but aside from that he keeps his thoughts of world domination to himself. So I was surprised when I heard repeated meowing for no apparent reason. I was sitting on the sofa, trying to finish a purchase request before I had to leave for the doctor's office. A hard rain was coming down when I heard the knock. Finn flew into the living room and flashed me an I-tried-to-warn-you look as I opened the front door. A pleasant-looking couple, a white man and a Black woman, greeted me warmly as they dripped onto my front porch. I was holding Finn in my arms lest he attempt to bolt into the great outdoors (he is always seeking ways to expand his empire.)

I'm never rude to Jehovah's Witnesses because a) meanness is bad, b) their dedication is admirable, c) I enjoy arguing, and d) I have great fondness for my daughter's lapsed Mormon ex-boyfriend. I can't stand the thought of anyone being mean to Kameron even though he's non-practicing and didn't do his mission and was never a Jehovah's Witness. Clutching my glowering cat, I listened politely as the Jay-Dubyas shared a Scripture from the book of James with me, the gist of which was that if bad things happen, it isn't God who did it to you. I told them honestly that I agree with that, but inwardly I was a wee bit shaken by their timing considering I was on my way to the *cancer doctor.*

After politely informing my visitors that I needed to get to an appointment, I closed the door and had a wee convo with the Big Guy.

"Really, God? I see you standing there with your hands up, all 'don't blame me.'"

God put his hands down, but I could tell He was still smirking.

"Your sense of humor is not all that funny sometimes. Stop giggling. And wipe that smile off your face. Geez."

My appointment was a follow-up to the appendix incident from the previous year. A surgeon had removed my appendix a few months after it ruptured and had found a tumor on it which they assured me was benign. Apparently, Dan Quayle had the same kind. Great, I always wanted to have something in common with Dan Quayle. My appointment was a follow up to ensure my tumor still wasn't cancerous. The head of surgical oncology informed me that the chance of my benign tumor becoming cancerous was in the single digits. I reminded him the chance of my appendicitis being caused by a tumor was less than 1 percent and that happened.

Still, I felt only a little worried as I headed out into the chilly rain and drove myself to the hospital. I circled the parking deck, found the right floor in the Cancer Center, checked in on an iPad, and grabbed one of those buzzers they use in restaurants to let you know your table is ready. After reciting my date of birth and providing my electronic signature a few dozen times, I sat in a large waiting room until summoned to a smaller waiting room.

There, a chatty, hair-free woman in a pink baseball cap began telling me her life story. I listened attentively because (see above.) She told me the names of her great-grandchildren that live with her. She recounted how she had watched her husband take his last breath twelve years ago after he collapsed from a blood clot following back surgery. She shared how and when she was diagnosed with cancer and the tough time she had with chemo at the beginning.

She was a sweet woman, and I listened and smiled and asked her questions. But inwardly I was screaming *I'm not one of you! You think I am, but I'm not! I don't have cancer!* There was an invisible line separating us and I hadn't crossed it. I know that makes me a terrible person, but I just wasn't mentally prepared.

At that moment, I thought of all the incarcerated women I'd known through the years from the weekly Bible study Holly and Becky I have led at the downtown jail on Tuesday nights. Once jailed, these women become less than human, just numbers in a system. Our goal was to make them feel like beloved daughters and provide them with a glimmer of hope for ninety minutes a week. Even after release, these women would be stigmatized for the rest of their lives. The Criminal vs. the Good Citizen. It was the same with cancer. There is a gulf between the Sick and the Well. Once you cross the line into Cancerland, you are separated from others. You become mortal: a patient, a sufferer, maybe a survivor. Your identity is subsumed by the illness.

As I silently freaked out about a cancer diagnosis, the lab techs took my blood, and the radiology techs ran me through the CT scanner, a painless yet eerie procedure which made me feel like I was on a Star Trek episode. In yet another waiting room, I worked on a jigsaw puzzle of a lighthouse while waiting to see the physician's assistant who would tell me my scan results. A woman next to me talked loudly on her phone, describing the intensive surgery/chemo combination informally known as "shake and bake" that her husband would be undergoing for appendiceal cancer. This harrowing procedure involves an incredibly long surgery to scrape away any potentially cancerous mucous attached to your organs, followed by a "chemo bath" where they swish poisonous chemicals around your innards for a couple of hours hoping to kill any random cancer cells. I knew I could be facing the same procedure.

The cancer P.A. Stephanie was saying "everything looks fine" as she entered the room and headed to the sink to wash her hands. Relieved that I was still in the Land of the Well, I asked a few more questions and headed out the door, off to thoughtlessly live my life for another year until the next follow-up appointment. The woman who checked me out of the Cancer Center noticed where I worked and asked me if I knew her brother, an IT instructor at the college. In fact, I did—a nice and helpful colleague. She spoke softly and kindly to me, and I wanted to blurt out "I don't have cancer," but I didn't. I walked out of the oncology clinic, head down with eyes averted, not wanting to make eye contact with anyone left in the waiting area in case I looked too happy. I hurried to my car in the parking deck, called Craig with the good news, and drove to campus, back to my normal workaholic ways. I put cancer and death into a small mental compartment and filed it into the very back of my brain somewhere between trigonometry and the names of my kindergarten friends.

The next day, a ding in my inbox alerted me to a new test result in my online health portal. The ability to see medical test results as they pop into your account is a mixed blessing. I read medical jargon about as well as I read French; I understand 50 percent of the words and occasionally can process an entire sentence. However, it was clear that a score of 15.6 on a tumor marker test where the normal range is between three and five is probably not a good thing. I shot a message to the P.A. and began to frantically Google each word in the report.

As I feared, Stephanie agreed that my bloodwork was "not good" and scheduled me for a PET scan eight days hence. Thus began my second period of preparing for imminent death, the first being the year before when they told me they had found a tumor on my appendix. A quick brush with death was one thing; a long uncertain slog of suffering was another.

Craig accompanied me to the hospital for the PET scan. He hummed nervously as they pumped radioactive dye into my veins to light up any cancerous spots in my body during the scan. After waiting an hour for the radioactive material to circulate, I was laid in a large plastic tray and my body was passed in and out of the whirring donut. There were sparkly butterflies on the ceiling and a computerized voice told me when to inhale, hold, and exhale my breath. I scanned the face of the kind technician, wondering if she could tell what the scan shows as she runs it. Was she being so nice to me out of pity or was she just nice to everyone? Unable to read her face, I got dressed and Craig and I headed upstairs to get the results.

Stephanie-the-PA bounded into the room and clicked on the computer scrolling through what was apparently a head-to-toe scan of my body.

"We don't see anything," she said. "I've conferred with Dr. Levine and the scan looks clear."

"Wow. That was not what I expected," I say slowly, mentally travelling back to the land of the living.

"Me neither," was her startling response.

"I can go to Ireland next weekend?"

"Yes. Go live your life. Come back in six months."

Getting the reprieve was a surprise. I'd been expecting to cancel the trip, my mind busy with planning my funeral. Now I wasn't going to die, *and* I got to go to Ireland.

I know we're not supposed to have favorites, but Ireland is my favorite. It's my happy place. My DNA says I'm about five percent Irish, forty percent if you count Scots Irish, but I'm not sure that has anything to do with my love for the Emerald Isle. It's the place I've returned to the most. Some people love baking in the sun on a sandy beach with a fruity drink with an umbrella. I prefer sipping an Irish coffee next to a cozy fire on a gray and rainy day. The shades of green that result from the rain, the foggy mists swirling around ancient stones, the stunning cliffs and crumbling castles, the frequent rainbows lazing above ubiquitous sheep are all balms for my soul.

The Irish are storytellers and poets, with more Nobel prizes in literature than any other country. The ancient Celtic myths and legends recorded by early monks are still widely known even by Irish millennials. It's a land of stories, including many tragedies. The Irish struggled under centuries of oppressive British rule, through starvation and emigration during the Great Hunger, and from the bombs and tit-for-tat retaliation of the Troubles. Tough as nails, and charming as hell. I love the Irish as much as I love their country.

My first visit to Éire was in 2006 when I abandoned my students to stalk Bono with my husband and kids. Three years later, Craig and I returned to Dublin to celebrate our twentieth anniversary by seeing U2 play at Croke Park to their hometown crowd. Watching the boys play in Dublin was unforgettable. The 82,000 people in the stadium all seemed to have walked to the venue. After the show, we poured into the streets, singing as we walked back to our homes and hotels. Five years later, we returned to Ireland to celebrate my fiftieth birthday. We considered other destinations, but somehow, we ended up back in Ireland. I loved the idea of spending my birthday in a castle. We stayed in a courtyard room at Cabra Castle in County Cavan, stone inner walls and wooden beams encasing us with medieval protectiveness. An Irish Wolfhound named Oscar lounged on the castle steps and roamed the grounds. Suits of armor and roaring fires were scattered around the main castle.

I also managed to finagle a private invitation to Slane Castle in County Meath with an email saying it was my birthday and that my maiden name was Cunningham. I'm not sure why they allowed me and Craig to come when the castle was closed to the public, but we got a lovely private tour from extremely gracious people. The castle belongs to the Conyngham family, Scots who were given the land in the 1600s as part of the Ulster Plantation when England schemed to make Ireland less Irish by populating the island with good English and Scottish Protestants. The original Lord Conyngham had twenty-nine children, and it's probable that I'm a long-lost poor relation. My aunt traced our Cunningham family back to Ramelton, a town in County Donegal, about a hundred miles northwest of Slane.

Slane Castle sits in the Boyne Valley, minutes away from Newgrange, a neolithic passage tomb older than Stonehenge and the Egyptian pyramids. I strolled through the castle, looking for family resemblances in the photos scattered about. The Cunningham motto Over Fork Over was proudly displayed over the fireplace. I was especially thrilled to see the drawing room where U2 recorded *The Unforgettable Fire* in 1984 and the ballroom where they filmed a video for their song *Pride (In the Name of Love)*. In 2001, the band performed to a sold out crowd on the castle grounds as part of their Elevation Tour. A few other minor bands and artists (The Rolling Stones, Queen, Bob Dylan, Bruce Springsteen, the Red Hot Chili Peppers, and REM, for example) have also played concerts at Slane Castle.

The Ireland trip following my medical reprieve was my seventh visit to the Emerald Isle, and my fourth time in Bundoran, the "Surf Capital of Ireland" on the northwest coast in County Donegal. In 2015 we received a small grant to create a spring break study abroad program in Ireland, a perfect destination for community college students' first international experience. Relatively close to the U.S., Ireland is a friendly and welcoming English-speaking country. There are enough cultural differences to make it interesting, but not so many that students freak out. (Well, they do freak out when they order a dessert with whipped cream and find out it's unsweetened. Another student fell in love with the croissants at breakfast, assuming they were an Irish food since she'd never had them in North Carolina.) We've run the program every year for almost a decade and every single participant loves Ireland. It's a sure bet.

It helps that we have phenomenal partners, a pair of work spouses named Niamh (pronounced *Neeve*) and John. In addition to being a Bundoran native, Niamh has a PhD in Irish Studies and is an incredible lecturer. Students are mesmerized as she recounts Irish history from the Stone Age to the present day, making connections between Ireland and issues in the States. Students especially love it when Niamh leads them in an Irish singsong, playing her guitar and teaching them tunes about Molly Malone, the Wild Rover, and the Hills of Donegal. John is silver-haired, knowledgeable and kind, and always smells fantastic. After a morning lecture, Niamh and John take the students to see related sites: from St. Patrick's well to the ruins of a Franciscan Abbey to the city of Derry in Northern Ireland, where the British army shot twenty-six unarmed protestors on Bloody Sunday in 1972.

On this occasion, Niamh and John had invited me to present at a faculty development seminar designed to convince other community college faculty and administrators from around the U.S. to bring students to Bundoran. I had been in Ireland with students six months earlier over spring break. I felt a little guilty about getting another trip to Ireland in exchange for a couple of presentations, but hey, it's nice work if you can get it. The day the group went to Derry, I asked if I could stay behind. My knee was killing me (I had it replaced a month later), I had been to Derry multiple times, and I wanted a little alone time, hoping the location would inspire me to write.

For lunch, I hobbled to a sandwich shop down the street that Niamh recommended. I sat at a small table at the back, not sure if I should order at the counter or if they had table service. A server arrived and I could sense people's ears perk up when they heard my American accent. It wasn't crowded but there was a steady stream of customers. After I paid my bill, I tried to stand up and fell on my ass. Legendary. I thought I was scooting out of a booth, but the booth ended like a cliff edge for Wile E. Coyote. The handful of people in the café who had been eyeing me curiously rushed to my rescue. With nothing wounded except my pride, I managed to limp back to the aparthotel.

The next day, we stopped at Drumcliffe in County Sligo on the way back to Dublin. St. Columcille built an abbey on the site in the sixth century. There is a beautiful high cross, the remains of a round tower, and a charming tea house and gift shop. The church which now stands there is no longer Catholic, but rather Church of Ireland. Under stained glass windows, the rector sat our group down in the front pews and regaled us with the long, but vivid story of the Battle of the Book. Though Columcille is the patron saint of County Donegal and is credited with bringing Christianity to the north of Ireland, he was no saint. He killed a few people and secretly copied an illuminated book of psalms while visiting his friend St. Finnian. Finnian was not happy when he found out and demanded that Columcille return the copy to him. Columcille refused and thus began the Battle of the Book. Ultimately, Diarmaid, the High King, ruled that the book had to be returned to Finnian with this proclamation: "To every cow its calf, to every book its child-book," thus establishing the notion of copyright. This is the very short version of the story because I'm only five percent true Irish.

The church boasts a charming graveyard, and several Cunninghams are buried at Drumcliffe. However, the most famous person lying here by far is Nobel-prize winning poet William Butler Yeats, who chose to be buried in the shadow of the mountain Ben Bulben. Snapping a photo at Yeats' grave is a must for visitors. His tombstone is engraved with his famous self-penned epitaph:

Cast a cold eye
On life, on death.
Horseman, pass by!

On this visit, the epitaph hit me extra hard, my brush with death refusing to stay in the dusty back corner of my mind to which I'd relegated it. I've read a lot of interpretations of Yeats' lines and none of them strike me as exactly right. I hate the idea that poetry is subject to interpretation and means what you want it to mean. I loved one of my graduate school professors who would listen to students' opinions and then say "No, that's not right at all." After she explained it, we all nodded in agreement that there was no other possible interpretation. But here's how I interpret Yeats' lines: Look at both life and death objectively and even dispassionately. Know that life will go on without you and that you will go on without life. I was glad the Horseman had passed me by for now.

The lines on Yeats' tombstone are the last words of a much longer poem called *Under Ben Bulben*. Here's the part I like best:

Many times, man lives and dies
Between his two eternities,
That of race and that of soul,
And ancient Ireland knew it all.
Whether man dies in his bed
Or the rifle knocks him dead,
A brief parting from those dear
Is the worst man has to fear.

Ah, the Irish. They always know the right thing to say. I never feel more alive than when I'm travelling, especially in Ireland.

SOUTH AFRICA: HERE AT THE END OF ALL THINGS

Six months of chronic diarrhea wasn't going to stop me from going to Africa. For decades, Africa had been at the top of my wish list, and even though I checked off the continent in 2004 when I spent a day in Morocco, that didn't really count in my mind. North Africa is part of the MENA region (Middle East and North Africa), distinct from the rest of the continent. I'd learned a lot about the MENA region by being the American mom to students and Fulbright FLTAs from Morocco, Egypt, and Tunisia. For several years, our college was selected to host Tunisian students through the Thomas Jefferson Scholarship Program. Created following the Jasmine Revolution in 2011, which brought democracy to Tunisia and kicked off the Arab Spring, the program was designed to strengthen relations between our countries and train young Tunisians to become leaders in the workforce.

It came as no shock to me that virtually no one at my rural North Carolina college had the slightest idea where Tunisia is. Occasionally, a student would tentatively raise a hand and suggest "North Africa?" in a quavering voice. I wanted to jump up and hug that young person, my faith in the future of humanity momentarily restored. Sadly, that was rare. Others regularly confused the country with Tanzania, while some thought Tunisia was a Caribbean island.

More than once, the students were asked: "If you're from Africa, why aren't you Black?" A *faculty member* in the automotive program told a female student that she could write an essay about the digestive system of a camel since she didn't own a car. I was incensed, but the student didn't want to cause trouble by filing a complaint. I constantly quoted Eleanor Roosevelt to the international students: "You can curse the darkness, or you can light a candle."

They were country ambassadors, sharing their culture with people who had never even heard of them. They were there to educate as much as they were there to gain an education. Over the years, our Tunisians and other Muslim students changed the campus culture. People grew accustomed to hearing Arabic spoken and attitudes about Muslims changed once people actually knew a Muslim. Not every student can go abroad, but I could bring the world to them. At a university, you're unlikely to find a job that works with inbound (international) *and* outbound (study abroad) students, but one perk of wearing all the hats is witnessing all the joy.

My Tunisian students were just like my bio kids—I loved them, and they drove me crazy in equal measure. They were all smart and funny and almost always ran late. Some of the students were more Western and others were more conservative. One student wore a hijab; another didn't. One student would keep *halal* (a challenge in the rural South); another tried bacon. I learned about *harissa*; they learned about biscuits and grits. Our cultures blended beautifully in a Bojangles' Cajun Fillet chicken biscuit. One of my fondest memories is of Dhia practicing his Irish language skills with Rita, our fabulous Fulbright Foreign Language Teaching Assistant from Ireland. There's nothing new under the sun, but a Tunisian speaking Irish at a rural North Carolina community college has got to be unique. This was one of those banal miracles.

The students were always on my mind, even when sedated. Following a colonoscopy, I opened my eyes a crack and squinted at my husband, coming out of my glorious propofol-induced sleep.

"Did I say anything weird?" I ask.

"You were talking about Tunisians," he informs me.

"Figures," I reply.

Having these precious students to care for helped fill my empty-nest heart. I wish I hadn't been quite so busy or stressed. Wearing all the hats can be exhausting. I was so focused on making sure the students met the requirements of their program, that I didn't take enough time to simply enjoy them. I have fond memories of each of them but regret not just hanging out more. While I've yet to travel to Tunisia, I did make it to sub-Saharan Africa with my bio fam.

So back to the diarrhea.

I constantly looked at ways to create a study abroad program in Africa, but it can be a hard sell to students due to distance, cost, and misconceptions. Finally, my friend Nadine and I wrote a grant to create a service-learning program in South Africa. We made a connection with Mike and Desi at EDU Africa who run top-quality but affordable study abroad programs. Their service-learning program in Cape Town was just what we were looking for. The grant included a site visit for me and Nadine to vet the program and meet with service-learning providers in different communities. Site visits were the absolute best part of my job: international travel without being responsible for a group of people. Unfortunately, site visits were rare since they were only possible through grants.

I was excited about this trip in a way I hadn't been for a long time. While travel still was a balm for my heart and mind, the novelty had worn off. My bad knees and aching hip made the actual travel part even more unpleasant. But I was thrilled to go to South Africa despite the back-to-back long-haul flights. I was a little worried about the diarrhea. I'd paid an eighty-dollar co-pay to a gastroenterologist to tell me I had "diarrhea of unknown origin." Thanks, doc. At least he told me that

Imodium is a near-perfect drug and that I could take as much as I wanted for as long as I wanted. Problem solved. Having never had chronic diarrhea of unknown origin, I did worry that it might be related to my elevated tumor marker, but I stuffed that to the back of my mind. Mostly.

It was a special year for our family: Anna graduated from college, Daniel received his Master of Divinity degree, and Craig and I were celebrating thirty years of marital *bliss*. I convinced Craig we needed "one last family vacation" to celebrate all these events. We considered Croatia or Greece, but I had enough frequent flyer miles to get the family to South Africa since the grant was paying my way. Nadine and EDU Africa assured me it was okay to bring them (for a reasonable fee), so we set our sights on the Rainbow Nation. Going with the kids to Africa was a double blessing. I missed them and having the nuclear family together in a place I'd always dreamed of visiting made my heart doubly warm. Especially with the Sword of Damocles (cancer) hanging over my head.

Best of all, I didn't have to fly all that way with Craig since the grant paid for my flights and he and the kids were routed differently using my miles. The kids would have to deal with his unbearable grouchiness due to flying anxiety and I could keep my window seat. Craig was especially nervous about flying over the Middle East, worried that ISIS would shoot us down and behead us. We told him not to worry—we would most certainly die when we hit the ground.

Craig and the kids flew out of Charlotte to Chicago while Nadine and I departed from Raleigh to Boston. We crossed paths in the airport in Doha, Qatar. Craig looked like an angry neglected circus bear and scowled and grunted when I asked him if he'd seen the flight map when we were midway between Baghdad and Tehran. My grown children looked at me with desperation in their eyes and begged for money for a snack since Craig had refused them. Feeling sorry for the poor little grownups, I handed over some cash and waved goodbye with a chipper smile. Nadine and I grabbed an Uber to explore a night market in Doha while my family flew on to Johannesburg. Yes, this was working out perfectly.

As we stepped out of the airport, the air was stifling; the average daily high in Doha is 108° in July with a low of 88°. We were giddy on the short ride to the Souq Waqif night market, from the long flights and our first glimpse of the Middle East. We strolled through shops selling heavy gold necklaces and colorful cloth. I bought a crêpe from two young women seated outside in white plastic chairs. My rule of thumb allows me to count Qatar as a country I've visited: if you eat something outside the airport, it counts. The women wore long black abayas and head scarves in the thick night. I couldn't imagine wearing those heavy clothes during the sizzling daytime. They smiled at us shyly, apparently unaccustomed to seeing a white American woman and a Black American woman strolling together through the square around midnight. Did they think we were crazy? Did they admire our freedom? Did they find us shameless? Whatever they thought, I'm sure we were an unusual sight.

All five of us arrived in Cape Town shortly before noon. Nadine and I had flown directly from Doha, while the family had an added leg through Joburg. (My miles only got them that far. We had to purchase the last leg to Cape Town.) It was a cool winter July day, and we were greeted warmly by Frans, who would soon become part of the family. Fransie (rhymes with Fonzie) was a driver by weekday and a pastor on the weekend. He had an infectious smile that exuded deep warmth and sincerity. He took to calling Craig "Pops" which made me and the kids giggle. He was used to Americans, so he didn't blink at Anna's tattoos and nose rings, even though she did get some looks in other places.

As we left the airport in the EDU Africa van and headed toward downtown, we began to see shanties, or shacks, as the South Africans call them without any pejorative intent. We passed by the township of Langa, which Craig and I would tour later in the week. Langa means "Sun" in Xhosa, which is one of South Africa's eleven official languages. I love listening to Xhosa, but my attempt to learn any consists of watching one YouTube video demonstrating the basic click sounds. As we left the suburbs and entered downtown, our surroundings changed dramatically— we were suddenly in a modern and attractive city with all the restaurants, shops, and coffee houses one would expect to see in Europe or the United States.

The first place Fransie took us was to a coffee shop where caffeine and sugar perked us from our long trip. My kids are coffee culture fans. In fact, both were using their college degrees to make lattes and cappuccinos. Anna had been working at Starbucks for a while, which Daniel disdains, as he works at a hipster gourmet coffee company in Raleigh. While in South Africa, the two of them got to do a cupping—a coffee tasting—at Origin Coffee. Known for their artisan roasting skills and barista training, Origin even had a barista go to the World Championships. Who knew baristas had world championships?

From the coffee shop, we drove to the top of Signal Hill and got our first stunning view of the city. We could see both Lion's Head and Table Mountain—the two iconic peaks overlooking the city. The clouds and late afternoon sunshine were dramatic and playful. I felt like Moses on the mountaintop, sure that the face of God was about to show itself. Table Mountain's flat top was covered in fog, known as its "tablecloth," but we could see everything else clearly: the Atlantic Ocean, the city center, the harbor, and the stadium built for the 2010 World Cup which can hold more than 64,000 fans. The magic of standing on a wind-swept peak in Africa with my family was overwhelming.

I may have been an imperfect wife and mother, I thought, *but if nothing else, I brought you to this amazing place.* While I sometimes worry that I've spoiled my children, I have nothing but gratitude for the time we spent in South Africa. Witnessing the spectacular natural beauty and getting to know remarkable South Africans was the gift of a lifetime.

Each day was filled with wonder. From sipping Pinotage at beautiful wineries to watching African Penguins surf at Boulder Beach, to strolling through a lion sanctuary (a possible service-learning location for our Zoo & Aquarium students), each activity was more thrilling than the last. At the Cape of Good Hope on the southwestern most point of Africa, we snapped photos while wild baboons scampered around us. In a home in the Bo Kaap neighborhood—a street of brightly colored houses occupied by the descendants of Muslim slaves brought over during British and Dutch rule—a lovely woman gave us a cooking lesson. In an authentic African restaurant, we tried crocodile, springbok, kudu, and ostrich. Another restaurant called Gold featured a fourteen-course dinner with dishes from all over the continent in addition to a lavish show.

As a possible activity for our nursing students, we visited the Grute Schoor Hospital where Dr. Christiaan Barnard had performed the world's first heart transplants. Everything was recreated in creepy plastic likenesses, except for the actual hearts from the first six transplants, which were displayed in large, murky jars.

In addition to the cultural activities, we spent time in the townships, getting to know our service-learning providers. We visited Khayelitsha, Cape Town's largest township with a population of more than a million people, one of the five largest slums in the world. We toured Baphumelele, a non-profit in the heart of Khayelitsha which serves the 14,000 orphans living there ,in addition to providing services to those infected with HIV/AIDS.

We discussed the multiple serving opportunities for students there and observed a class of four-year-olds, where adorable kids behaved like four-year-olds everywhere. We visited an even rougher township called Ocean View where Johann, who runs a non-profit there, told us about the four- and five-year-olds in his neighborhood. When the children first start coming to his program, they are listless and easy to manage. However, once they start getting food on a regular basis, they begin to act like miniature gangsters—mimicking the violence they've witnessed daily in their young lives. It takes a lot of work for them to adjust their behavior to what one might expect from normal preschoolers. The trauma they've experienced before the age of five will never be fully healed.

Craig and I took a half-day tour of Langa while Nadine and our kids hiked Table Mountain. Created in 1927, Langa is the oldest of the townships to which Black Africans were forced to move after the Urban Areas Act of 1923. Many people were relocated to Langa from District Six in the pre-Apartheid era. Our personal guide Nela walked us through the streets of the township and explained the history. The first thing we saw was the housing where white authorities controlled the settlement when it was built. From there, we moved to a street of rundown shops where the word *Ubuntu* was painted on an old Coca-Cola sign above a locked storefront.

According to Archbishop Desmond Tutu, the word *Ubuntu* means "the essence of being human. Ubuntu speaks particularly about the fact that you can't exist as a human being in isolation. It speaks about our interconnectedness....We think of ourselves far too frequently as just individuals, separated from one another, whereas you are connected and what you do affects the whole world."

As we walked through the poorest section of the neighborhood, tears filled my eyes. It was unfathomable that hundreds of millions of people live this way. I had seen plenty of poverty in South and Central America, but the sheer scale of it in the townships was overwhelming. I was also filled with shame; here I was a middle-class American white lady touring this place as just another stop on the itinerary. I apologized to our guide for my tears and asked him his opinion about poverty tourism. He told me not to be embarrassed, that he could see my heart and that the money we paid for the tour was helping the community. Still there was a hardness in his face. I imagined he'd met many Americans whose eyes filled with tears, until they moved on to the wineries and safaris.

Many people question why God allows suffering; I worry that God will ask us why we allow it.

After taking a moment to compose myself, we entered a small wood and tin shack. Sunlight streamed through the wood frame of a window half covered by a curling tarp. Around the perimeter of the small room, men with lined faces and baseball caps sat on rough benches. There was just enough room for us to squeeze in. Our guide told us we were in a *shebeen*, a word which comes from Irish but does not in any way resemble any pub I've ever been in. Nela purchased a metal bucket of Umqombothi, a beer made of maize and sorghum, brewed by local women over an open fire. He passed the bucket around and everyone in the shack took a gulp of the gritty, frothy liquid. The mood was not festive, and we left the rest of the pail for the men to pass around.

As we exited the *shebeen*, we passed another ramshackle space strewn with log stumps, plywood, cardboard, and white plastic buckets. Nela pointed out what we didn't observe at first: a dozen sheep heads piled on a sagging board toward the back of the space. This staple of the Langa diet is "smileys;" the sheep heads are seared over an open flame and then boiled, dramatically revealing the teeth, which appear to be smiling (or grimacing in pain and terror). One head can feed a family of five with the ears, eyes, and tongue considered to be the tastiest parts. I considered my own willingness to eat meat only if it doesn't resemble an animal.

Toward the end of our tour, we visited Nela's grandmother's house—a small but neat brick house in a row of small, neat houses. Perhaps more than anything, these homes surprised me. I had assumed that all the houses would be shacks; it hadn't occurred to me that there would be people who chose to live in Langa when they could have afforded to move out. Teachers and nurses and other professionals lived in this part of the township, and it had a strong middle-class vibe. The final part of the tour included a visit to an artist co-op where I guiltily purchased several items while simultaneously thinking "Geez, these prices are high." Oh, the hypocrisy.

After a selfie with Nela and slipping him a generous tip, we met Fransie who drove us to the Victoria & Albert waterfront to wait for our children and Nadine to finish climbing Table Mountain. We walked through the western-style mall, had a drink on an outdoor patio, perused gift shops, and looked at the photos of prisoners on the wall at the Robben Island ferry. We had been disappointed when the water was too rough for us to visit Mandela's prison cell a few days earlier, but I consoled myself with the thought that I would go next year with students. Who knew that in sixth months we would begin hearing about a virus in Wuhan China that would soon affect the entire world?

The hours went by, and we waited for a call from Fransie. Surely, they would be finished hiking soon. The Table Mountain cable car was being repaired, so the kids and Nadine had to hike up *and* down the steep peak. It was almost dark when Fransie drove us to the pickup point. Nadine was down and Anna arrived soon after. I was starting to panic as it grew darker, and Daniel still didn't arrive. I had thought Nadine was going to stay with them (as did they), but she regarded them as adults, capable of taking care of themselves. Daniel finally arrived in an exhausted rage; he thought he might die on the mountain. It took a full day for him to recover from the trauma, but ultimately, he was glad he had done it and would even do it again, if he had the proper shoes.

Nadine decided to spend some time in Jo-burg on her way home, so she headed off to the Cape Town airport while the LaVentures headed to the Aquila game reserve. We splurged on the overnight excursion, partly because it would be included in the student program and partly because it seemed mandatory for a trip to Africa. Shortly after checking into our lodge, we boarded a large jeep-like vehicle and headed out to see the animals. We drove past elephants sucking up water from shallow pools. We squinted to see giraffes and zebras camouflaged by the terrain. Cape buffalo and springbok and kudu dotted the landscape. Herds of hippos and rhinos passed in front of us with their portly babies. The lions lived in a fenced-off area, but we drove through the gate and parked right next to them—two brothers and their three wives. Delighted, I mentally shouted "Kitties!" while Craig looked around nervously, assessing which of us he would throw to the lions if the chubby cats started looking hungry.

The next morning's sunrise game drive was a complete bust: I forced Craig and the kids out of bed in the dark only to endure a cold and rainy drive around the plains without sighting so much as a jack rabbit. Everyone was a little cranky on the long drive back to Cape Town. Mike and Desi were surprised that we hadn't loved Aquila—it's usually a big hit with all the student groups. We complained about the price and how the food wasn't all that great. Suddenly, I realized we were whiny, ungrateful wankers who needed a kick in the ass. How could I go from crying about the way people live in the townships to bitching about how our luxury safari wasn't as fantastic as we expected? Geez. I was a legendary *asshole*.

I take comfort in the stories from the Bible that remind me that I am not the only ungrateful asshole who ever lived. In fact, it's the human condition. Consider the Israelites rescued from 400 years of slavery who crossed the sea on dry ground and ate manna provided fresh each morning. They began griping almost immediately about how they wished they could have just stayed in Egypt. King David, "a man after God's own heart," committed adultery with Bathsheba and ordered her husband to the front lines knowing he would be killed. Jonah was so pissed off that the evil Ninevites turned to God after he preached repentance that he sat under a tree and wished he could die. Jonah is my favorite. I'd be pissed, too.

It's important to remember that God knows we're assholes and loves us anyway.

As I contemplated my own outrageous and grotesque thoughts, the words of my favorite verse of my favorite hymn came to me.

Oh, to grace how great a debtor
Daily I'm constrained to be
Let Thy goodness, like a fetter
Bind my wandering heart to Thee
Prone to wander, Lord, I feel it
Prone to leave the God I love
Here's my heart, oh take and seal it
Seal it for Thy courts above [2]

I am prone to wander, but as Gandalf taught us, not all who wander are lost. In fact, wandering helps me find myself. Grace follows me around, overlooking my idiocy and selfishness. The

---

2 "Come, Thou Fount of Every Blessing," Robert Robertson, 1758

more I wander, the more I understand *Ubuntu*, the belief in a universal bond that connects all humans. When I meditate on the importance of interconnectedness, my obsession with control and perfection diminishes. The empty spaces fill up. I find joy in others: my family, my friends, and the people I meet around the world.

I am because we are.

HOME - A FAR GREEN COUNTRY

Sam and Frodo flee Mount Doom as it erupts after absorbing the One Ring in the film, *The Return of the King*. The hobbits run along stone arches that fall away into the fiery lava below as they cross them. Exiting the mouth of the cave, they leap onto a tall boulder as rivers of molten rock flow underneath them. As they lie exhausted on the rock while death and devastation surge about them, they reminisce about the Shire: the Brandywine River, Gandalf's fireworks, Rosie Cotton dancing with ribbons in her hair. They think of home and of what might have been. As Sam laments the fact that he'll never get to marry Rosie, Frodo comforts his friend without false reassurances: "I'm glad to be with you Samwise Gamgee, here at the end of all things."

I didn't plan on being diagnosed with a rare and deadly form of appendix cancer in the middle of a global pandemic. As I lay on a figurative rock contemplating my imminent death, the country erupted around me with unprecedented everything: quarantine, revolution, racial reckoning. As weird as it sounds, receiving my diagnosis during those terrible times was oddly reassuring. Everyone on the planet was facing the daily threat of death and the disorienting effects of an unknown future. The world wasn't spinning on without me, people weren't going on with their busy lives while my life came to a standstill. It was a terrible time for everyone. Maybe it's an awful thing to admit, but there was comfort in not suffering alone.

Two months into the quarantine, I had gone to the hospital for my regular follow-up. My "scanxiety" was way lower than it had been during my quarterly visits the previous year. The process was now familiar: Sign in at the Cancer Center; get an IV inserted; undergo CT scan with contrast dye; meet with doctor to tell me my scan is clear; stop at labs on my way out for bloodwork. The moment I knew I had cancer was when a nurse came in and asked me to put on a gown. That had never happened before. Dr. Levine entered the room and asked me to hop onto the table so he could check out my abdomen.

"Does that hurt?" he asked as he pressed on my belly.

"No," I replied.

He offered his hand to help me sit up. As I returned to the plastic chair, he stood across the room and almost whispered: "Pseudomyxoma."

He knew I knew what that meant. He pegged me as a reader on our first meeting when I arrived with a folder of highlighted printouts of articles from various medical journals. He'd glanced at my collection of documents and waved his hand dismissively.

"Those are from crap journals," he said, which made me laugh.

Dr. Levine is one of the world's leading experts on this one-in-a-million disease. In addition to being one of the handful of surgical oncologists in the world who specialize in appendix cancer, he works at my hometown hospital, the one affiliated with my alma mater. People come from all over to be treated by him; I had a fifteen-minute drive to the hospital. Not only is he an imminent researcher, professor, and surgeon, but he's also friendly and upbeat, a dream doctor. A miracle in the shape of a man.

Pseudomyxoma Peritonei is a rare malignancy almost always originating in the appendix. Although the tumor they found on my appendix was benign, certain cells had escaped and were now secreting cancerous mucin (mucous) in my pelvis and abdomen. This explains how I was diagnosed with appendix cancer almost three years after a surgeon removed my appendix. The tiny mucin cells can attach themselves to any organ. Untreated, death within five years is almost certain. With treatment, the median survival is 9.8 years. The only effective treatment is cytoreductive surgery with HIPEC (Heated Intraperitoneal Chemotherapy.) This surgery/chemo combo is commonly referred to as MOAS—the Mother of All Surgeries. The operation lasts many hours as the surgeon tries to scrape every cell of mucin from the abdominal cavity. Following that, the body is filled with a heated chemotherapy "bath" for a couple of hours while the patient is jiggled on a vibrating table. *Shake and bake*. All this I knew.

"Okay," I responded upon receiving the diagnosis.

"Do you have any questions?"

I shook my head. None of the million questions I had previously scribbled in a notebook came to mind. We set a date for surgery for six weeks out.

"Start writing down your questions. I'll answer all of them at the pre-op visit the week before the operation."

"Thank you."

I walked dry-eyed to checkout and took the elevator down to labs for blood tests. I didn't feel the needle. Once I reached the parking deck, I ripped off the mask I'd been wearing for hours and fanned my sweating face with it. I called Craig from the car. He was upset; I felt nothing. As with most major events in my life, I felt detached, as if I were viewing myself from the outside. Marriage, childbirth, cancer. The realest things seem surreal to me.

Like Aragorn, I do not fear death. If I'm wrong about the afterlife, being dead doesn't seem so bad. It's just the very last item to check off my to do list. I did have a single sleepless night before the operation filled with existential dread about ceasing to exist. The thought of *not being* freaked me out, but daylight brought relief.

Here were the things I did fear: Pain and suffering. Ending up with a permanent colostomy bag. A long and difficult existence with poor quality of life. How my kids and Craig would cope. Missing my children's futures. Who would take care of my mom in her later years. Not being able to do my job. Dying before the final season of *Succession*. We live with the sense that we will go on forever until one day in old age, after everything has been accomplished, we will lie down and leave our desiccated bodies behind. When death comes zooming up in the rearview mirror like an asshole driver, you are forced to live in the present.

Between the pandemic and the cancer, it was a real possibility that my days of wandering were over. At the time, it was easy to envision a world where travel was a thing of the past, where I had been one of the last wanderers on Earth. Would we ever leave our homes again? Would we ever see white streaks of contrails in the sky again? Would international education be limited to virtual exchanges? Would the airline and travel industries disappear? The end of travel was more depressing than the end of me. I was satisfied that I had lived my life wide open, saying yes to the opportunities that came my way. I had facilitated travel for so many people who might never have traveled without my nagging persistence. Countless students testified "Mrs. LaVenture made me go," but were glad they went.

The world had changed me, and I had changed the world. What more can you ask for? I had no huge regrets.

I decided not to go public public (i.e. post on Facebook) with my diagnosis, but I did create a CaringBridge page for fifty or so of my closest friends. I was humbled by their effusive gestures of kindness. Believing I am loved has always been a struggle for me. More comfortable with giving than receiving, accepting that people truly cared for me was a difficult but amazing gift. My French friend Christèle drove from Maryland to visit me for a couple of hours. John and Niamh filmed a video of themselves tying a string to the pagan tree on my behalf next to St. Patrick's well in Donegal. Jason and Becca had a Mass said for me in Galway and Rosie lit candles at a church in Kilkenny. Jasim's mother in Iraq and Mike and Desi in South Africa were among those who prayed for me around the world. My faith was in the faith of my friends and family. I relied on their prayers much more than on my own. They sent soft blankets, meals, books, and bottles of wine.

Immensely grateful to the people close by and around the world who lifted me up and carried me through, I am blessed. My cup runneth over with friends. Regardless of the outcome of the surgery, I was a lucky woman.

At my pre-op appointment, Dr. Levine answered my lengthy list of questions.

"How long will the surgery last?"

"Eight hours. Or more."

"Which organs will you remove?"

"Anything you can do without."

"What kind of music do you listen to while operating?"

"Classic rock."

"How many people don't survive the surgery?"

"Three percent."

"Three percent! That seems awfully high!"

Levine shrugged. "You have to understand—it's the equivalent of exploding a bomb in your body."

Before dawn on a July morning, Craig drove me to the hospital. There were a surprising number of people in the waiting room. Elective surgeries were mostly cancelled, but apparently a lot of people needed some kind of essential operation. I'm fairly sure I was the only lucky one getting the Mother of All

Surgeries. Craig sat in the waiting room for the entire day, while I was mostly unconscious. They took me back to prep and soon I was knocked out while Dr. Levine scraped cancerous goo out of my peritoneal cavity and off my organs, removing my omentum, gall bladder, and reproductive organs in the process. I have no memory of being filled with liquid chemotherapy and vibrated like a washing machine.

Eventually a voice pierced my consciousness: "Can you tell me your name?"

"Suzanne LaVenture," I mumbled.

"Where are you?"

"Hospital."

"Which one?"

"Baptist."

"Can you tell me who the president is?"

"Don't make me say his name." I grimaced as if in great pain.

"It's okay. We know you know who it is."

The next morning a nurse asked me if I wanted to sit in the recliner, so I said yes. Apparently, this was an impressive feat. Others who came in were surprised to find me in the chair. As always, I was determined to be a good patient and recover faster than average. Dr. Levine had mentioned that my weight might make my recovery more difficult, so I was highly motivated to prove him wrong. The average stay in the hospital if there weren't any complications was a week to ten days; I went home on Day 6. Because I rock.

Because of COVID-19, I was allowed only one visitor for four hours a day. Both Craig and Anna were secretly happy about this. Craig sat with me faithfully for the four allotted hours and then returned home to care for the animals. Daniel came instead of Craig on one of the first days, but I was still mostly out of it. Anna was delighted to have an excuse not to visit me since she hates hospitals and faints at the sight of blood. She claims I didn't tell her how serious it was (possibly true) and that she feels bad about not visiting me. Knowing her phobias and under the circumstances, I really didn't mind that she didn't come to the hospital. However, I did want to show her my vertical line of bloody staples holding me together from my breastbone to my horizontal C-section scar, but I resisted. I don't want her to worry but I take great delight in grossing her out with my medical torture after the fact.

On the third day following surgery, I wanted to die. I assume they had cranked down the pain meds. I mentioned to Craig that maybe he could help me die if I had to endure this level of suffering for a prolonged period of time, a statement which shocked and appalled him. Whoops. My death wish only lasted a day; though I was still incapable of reading or watching TV or sending a coherent text, I improved. When they paroled me on Day Six, I too impatient to wait for a wheelchair, I walked out, not sure I would make it to the car. I still felt like hell. They told me a full recovery could take a year. I was worried about being at home without round-the-clock medical care, but Craig was a surprisingly good nurse. He even agreed to give me daily injections in my stomach for two weeks to prevent blood clots.

"I can't believe you agreed to give me belly shots," I said, pulling up my pajama top.

"I thought they said Jello shots," he quipped as he jabbed the needle in me.

We were lucky as far as the pandemic went—Craig and I both had jobs that went remote, meaning we still got paid and still had insurance. I couldn't imagine the double whammy of serious illness and financial devastation. My surgery cost close to $200,000, but we had to pay only a few thousand, thank God. It makes me furious that people can lose their life savings due to medical expenses. Recovering from surgery in a homeless shelter or on the streets is unimaginable, but many people must.

I was able to "go back to work" quickly since I was working from home and my workload was significantly reduced. All in all, I was very lucky in having Stage Four cancer during a global pandemic. I could afford it, my surgeon was kind and competent, and I had an amazing circle of support.

Many characters in *The Lord of the Rings* face seemingly imminent death. Pippin, another hobbit, prepares for a battle where the good guys are vastly outnumbered by an army of evil and terrifying creatures. In a calm moment before the fighting begins, he converses with the wizard Gandalf about their impending demise.

> PIPPIN: *I didn't think it would end this way.*
> GANDALF: *End? No, the journey doesn't end here. Death is just another path, one that we all must take. The gray rain curtain of this world rolls back, and all turns to silver glass, and then you see it.*
> PIPPIN: *What? Gandalf? See what?*
> GANDALF: *White shores, and beyond, a far green country under a swift sunrise.*
> PIPPIN: *Well, that isn't so bad.*

No, that isn't so bad. Venturing into the unknown has been the recurring motif of my life. Whether my cancer journey leads me to a miraculous rescue or to the far green country, I'm glad to be surrounded by a great fellowship, here at the end of all things.

BORDEAUX: *QUI VIVRA VERRA*

Iditched the students to spend the afternoon drinking Bordeaux in Saint-Émilion with Laura and her husband Alex. I didn't really ditch them. I left them in the capable hands of Owen and Lindley, who were leading the program on the ground, along with Thierry, our delightful French colleague. During my long recovery from the Mother of all Surgeries during the dark heart of COVID-19, I formed a relationship with partners at IUT-Bordeaux, the technical institute of the University of Bordeaux. We worked remotely to create a summer study abroad program in France based on entrepreneurship and technology. A grant subsidized the program for twenty community college students in the state of North Carolina to spend two weeks in Bordeaux. We originally hoped to run the program in 2021, but the pandemic refused to cooperate, and we took the first group of students in June of 2022.

Because of the capacity building nature of the grant, we sent four faculty from different colleges the first year: Owen, Laura, Jefferson and me. We arrived at the onset of a historic heat wave that included several days at 108° Fahrenheit. We're accustomed to heat in North Carolina, but we're also accustomed to air-conditioning. In France, A.C. was as scarce as hen's teeth. No air at the aparthotel, the university, restaurants. We passed a bar with a sidewalk blackboard proclaiming *"C'est chaud* AF," which became our motto. My student Genesis and I composed a song comparing the weather to various parts of Satan's body.

It helped. The temperature was miserable, but the students had good attitudes.

Each day, our students worked with French students at IUT-Bordeaux to create a solar-powered cell-phone charger which they would market to us Shark Tank-style at the end of the program. We faculty members took turns going with them to the university since they didn't really need four babysitters. Our only respite from the heat came when we were able to sneak away from the students and visit our secret place: le Bar à Vin. Located on the ground floor of Bordeaux's flatiron building, this wine bar offers a selection of thirty excellent wines by the glass at ridiculously low prices. Thierry and Luc took us there early during the two-week program, buying us several glasses of Crémant: sparkling wine from France made in the style of champagne that doesn't come from the Champagne region. We were hooked.

My colleagues and I made a habit of meeting at The Secret Place whenever the students were occupied, and our presence wasn't required. The chairs were comfy, the sommeliers pleasant and instructive. The wines were served in the correct kind of glass for each wine (as if I would know the difference). Le Bar à Vin even offered local delicacies to snack on: cheeses, meats, and chocolates. But I haven't even gotten to the best part: the AC was downright frigid. The place is popular with tourists, seeking to learn more about the region's vinous offerings, and they've created the perfect ambiance for Americans. Entering the chilly interior during the heat wave was like taking a step out of Hell into a glorious celestial icebox. Oh, how I enjoyed those days of wine and cheese and gossip, the icy AC drying the sweat on my back.

When the heat wave finally broke, a glorious rain poured from the sky. I caught some of the students dancing around like fools outside of the restaurant we were in. I didn't blame them. I was giddy with relief as well.

For the 2023 program, we reduced the number of faculty to three. I did most of the advance work: marketing the program, managing applications, communicating with students, teaching the pre-departure class. Owen and Lindley (who replaced Jefferson) were to be the primary leaders on the ground in France. Laura had left her job at a community college but brought her Spanish husband to Bordeaux just to visit for a few days during our program. It wasn't as hot, but we happily hit up our Secret Place on multiple occasions.

I was determined to enjoy the second Bordeaux program as much as possible, because it was going to be my last. No, I was not dying. My best friend NED (no evidence of disease) had shown up at all my follow-ups with Dr. Levine. But I was retiring. In 2021, the college won NAFSA's Senator Paul Simon award for comprehensive internationalization, perhaps the biggest international education award that exists. It was a big effin' deal.

Sadly, the new administration at the college did not seem to recognize the significance of the achievement. I kept waiting for them to acknowledge the work that not only I, but the many dedicated faculty and staff members on the International Education Committee had done. It was remarkable for a college, especially a community college, of our size and demographics to win this prestigious honor. Surely, they could send out an all faculty and staff email or mention it at one of the campuswide meetings.

Good thing I didn't hold my breath.

Nine months after notification of the award, our college was officially recognized at the NAFSA annual conference, which was held virtually that year. Several members of the Intl. Ed. Committee gathered for a watch party. I made a few snarky remarks when our president credited our success in international education to the Board of Trustees and the College Foundation.

Word got back to him, and I was summoned to a meeting with my boss, the big boss, and the biggest boss. I was raked over the coals for my comments without any acknowledgement that maybe they really should have publicly recognized us for winning such a big award.

I was completely dysregulated and tears streamed down my face throughout the meeting. I never cry, but I felt so shamed and humiliated that I couldn't help it. I apologized for my unprofessional comments though many things that were said to me in the meeting did not fit my definition of professionalism either. I was required to individually apologize to anyone who was at the watch party, which I did. Not a single person had any idea what I was apologizing for. Either they didn't hear my muttered comments, or they didn't see anything wrong with them.

Instead of being recognized for the decades of my life I had poured into the job, I was reprimanded. After the meeting, I sat outside the back of my building crying and shaking. As much as I wanted to quit in that instant, I'm no fool. I had close to two more years of work to reach thirty years of service, enough to receive a full pension for the rest of my life. I would suck it up and finish my time, though I wouldn't stay a minute more.

I would be just fifty-nine when I retired, but after that meeting I was done. Because I was grandfathered in to lifelong healthcare, I wouldn't have to work until sixty-five, the age of eligibility for Medicare. I kept my decision quiet until I filed my paperwork with the state three months before my retirement date. Even then, I kept it on the DL. I was worried about giving up the thing that had occupied most of my life for three decades. My identity was tied to my job—I was a renowned fish in the small pond of international education at community colleges.

What would it be like to not work every hour of every day? How would I function without my raison d'être? Would everything I'd worked so hard to achieve over the years dissipate into vapor when I left? Could I afford to travel on my own dime? On the other hand, I wouldn't miss my sixty-six-mile round trip daily commute. Some colleagues I would miss, others not so much. No more useless meetings, tedious paperwork, or frustrating dealings with the business office. No more beating my head against the wall trying to make people understand the importance of having a global perspective. Maybe retirement would do me good. Maybe I could fill my time in new ways. Maybe I would volunteer or get a part-time job. Maybe I would dust off the memoir I'd been working on.

My career had indeed been remarkable. It was a position I essentially created, with the support of like-minded faculty and staff. Like a mirage rising from the desert, I crafted my job from the mystical ingredients of stubborn passion and relentless hard work. My fierce belief in the need to show community college students the world was a powerful force. In a way, I feel sorry for my supervisors. Convinced of the rightness of my cause, I often refused to take no for an answer, either persisting in what I wanted until they agreed or finding a way around objections. I wasn't intentionally defiant; I just knew that people who opposed me simply didn't get it. (Okay, so maybe I was intentionally defiant.)

It just rarely crossed my mind that I needed to ask permission to do what obviously needed to be done.

I had come a long way from Cloister Drive. Who could have imagined my path would take me to more than forty countries on six continents? I was still an overweight, book-loving nerd, but I was also a legend! I'd found a way to fill up the holes inside me through travel and teaching and making a difference in students' lives. My childhood faith had not been extinguished but expanded. From the conga line in the Dominican Republic to the stark monasteries in Russia to the old ladies praying deep in the Amazon, the Spirit is the same. The style varies; the substance doesn't.

I was no longer a blind girl feeling a tusk and thinking I knew what an elephant was. I could see the whole animal from a variety of perspectives.

My body and I have reached something of a truce, too. I've started listening to it instead of pretending I exist in a floating head. If I have to pee, I get up and pee. When I'm hungry, I eat, and I try not to eat when I'm not hungry. When I'm tired, I rest. Sometimes I pat my leg and thank my body for everything it's done for me and all the places it's taken me. Getting older is something of a relief; the supermodel expectation has diminished, though it pisses me off when eighty-year-old Martha Stewart appears all sexy on a magazine cover. Can't we ever get a break from ridiculous beauty standards? Do we have to go to the grave worrying about wrinkles and flabby bits? My body is finally getting the recognition it deserves and less of the criticism I used to heap on it. I can see a future where we are friends.

I'm learning to live at peace with myself. I'm ready for a new adventure.

Laura, Alex, and I strolled about the ancient terroir of Château Canon-la-Gaffelière, ogling the mature vines loaded with baby grapes. We learned that the roses at the end of each row were not simply for decoration but served as "a canary in a coal mine," letting the vintners know if a problem was about to arise. Our private guide led us through the production facility and the barrel room. Finally, it was back to the tasting room where the three of us eagerly awaited our chance to sample the wines. We sat at a long wooden table in a dimly lit, medieval-looking room as our guide opened the wines. It was hard to believe that a mere three years earlier, I had been nervously awaiting massive surgery to treat my Stage Four appendix cancer.

At my most recent checkup with Dr. Levine, I mentioned my upcoming trip to Bordeaux. He began to discuss wine rather enthusiastically.

"I'll bring you a bottle," I told him. "For saving my life."

"Great, don't get anything cheap," he quipped.

"I won't," I laughed. "My life is worth a few euros."

Laura, Alex, and I savored the delicious wines, and I bought a bottle for Dr. Levine which I nestled carefully in a plastic sleeve I'd purchased. The wine warmed my insides as the sun on the French hillside warmed my soul. I thought fondly of our students at the university in Bordeaux, working side by side with their new French *amis*. I basked in the glow of friendship and adventure and red wine.

And as we walked back to the train station, I thought I could hear Bilbo Baggins singing faintly on the breeze, that the road goes ever on and on.

Photo by Craig LaVenture

ABOUT THE AUTHOR

Suzanne LaVenture is a world traveler, award-winning instructor, and a Fulbright Scholar. She created a program at Davidson-Davie Community College which won NAFSA's Senator Paul Simon Award for comprehensive internationalization. Suzanne has published articles in Diversity Abroad's *Global Impact Exchange*, *New Directions for Community Colleges*, and the *Journal of International Students*. She holds Spanish Language and Literature degrees from Wake Forest University (BA) and the University of Illinois (MA). She dabbles in other languages, including Arabic, French, Irish, and Elvish. She lives in Lewisville, NC with her husband Craig, and God's best cat Finn LaVenture.

ACKNOWLEDGMENTS

I'm so grateful to Sibylline Press for selecting this book for their Digital First Imprint launch. Their mission to give voice to older women is refreshing and much needed. It's been a lifelong dream of mine to publish a book, and the older you get, the tougher that dream becomes. Thanks to Publisher Vicki DeArmon, Executive Editor Julia Park Tracey, and the Sibylline team for making my dream come true. I'm tickled pink to be a Sibyl.

I offer many thanks to my sister, Dr. Cindy Cunningham, without whom this book would still be in a random Word file on my laptop. Her personal encouragement and professional advice, guidance, and editing made all the difference in making the publication of my memoir a reality. She's had to put up with me for her entire life, and I can be a lot. I'm delighted to have such a smart and talented little sister and thankful that she's so willing to help me.

I have been blessed to know many incredible people across the globe, who have made my life rich and meaningful. My memoir would be very dull without them. To every international student, scholar, or teaching assistant I've cared for—getting to know you has been one of the great joys of my life. You taught me much and left me with many memories of happy times. The same applies to my international friends. Dr. Niamh Hamill (brilliant) and John O'Connell (smells great) are almost entirely responsible for my lavish love of Ireland and are tremendous humans. Mike Massingham and Desiree Haakonsen are beautiful people and dear friends who showed me and my family the incredible heart and beauty of South Africa. Thierry Villard, thank you for your partnership and the best dinner I've ever had (food, company, and copious wine). I would expect no less from a Frenchman. I'd also like to thank Verónica Pellegrino in

Argentina and Irina Petrovska in Macedonia for being amazing Fulbright Scholars and incredibly gracious hosts. My travel experiences would not have been the same without you all. I can't leave out Dr. Mary Rittling who made my career possible by being a true believer in the power of travel to transform lives.

I am eternally grateful for my book club, a faithful family of female friends. I'll never forget them sneaking wine and snacks into my hospital room so I wouldn't miss our monthly meeting. I love you all. Thanks to long-time members Melissa Johnson for bacon sticks, Amanda Klinger for her Enneagram 8-ness, Julie James for being my friend for almost forever, Victoria Raczenski for being a hard-working millennial, Laura Hortal and Melissa Maley for pond time and wine time, Amanda Davis for being our second Math Amanda, Rebecca Boyd for healthy and tasty snack options, Janice Hauser for sharing her beautiful home and yard, and Helen Wyss for being all-around awesome even though it's unfair that she looks decades younger than me when it's only a couple of years. Also much love and thanks to Cat Drader, an OG book club member, and one of my first readers. Her humor, creativity, and exuberance have brought joy to my life.

Other important women in my life include Dr. Rosa Bird, a genius I have loved since our grad school days. Susan Triplett has been an invaluable and joyful presence in my life and, in some ways the unlikeliest of best friends. I loved seeing Christèle Cain at CCID conferences twice a year and I can't believe she drove from DC just to visit me when I was diagnosed with cancer. Nadine Russell has been my closest colleague and travel buddy—I enjoyed every minute with you from China to Ireland to Guatemala to South Africa. Never erase that video of us in the cab in Mexico.

Lastly, I'd like to thank Craig, my loving and supportive husband, my favorite son, Daniel, and my favorite daughter, Anna.

They are my preciouses. My cat Finn hasn't read the book, but I am thankful for his handsomeness and loud purring which have been a calming influence (even though it is not helpful to the writing process when he plops his pudgy primordial pouch on my keyboard.)

STUDY GUIDE QUESTIONS

1. How did the author's upbringing in a religious Southern household shape her worldview? In what ways did this background spark LaVenture's desire to travel?

2. How was the author's study abroad experience in Colombia a catalyst for the rest of the travels in her life?

3. Choose one of the destinations that stood out to you. How did the author bring the city or country to life? How did the author use details and story-telling to paint the picture?

4. In what way does Suzanne's cancer diagnosis fit into her travel memoir? In what ways did her international travel prepare her to face this challenge? Discuss the parallels between navigating new cultures and navigating illness.

5. How do the themes of faith, family, and exploration intertwine throughout the memoir? Would the memoir have been as successful without one of the elements? How so or why not?

6. How does the book's title resonate with the rest of the memoir?

7. What is the author's overall message about the importance of travel and cultural exchange? Do you agree?

8. Did the memoir inspire you to travel more? If you have ever traveled internationally, share a personal anecdote about an experience that challenged your perspective or broadened your worldview.

9. How did you respond to the author's voice? What role did humor play in the memoir? Do you think the author is trying to elicit a certain response or action from the reader?

www.ingramcontent.com/pod-product-compliance
Lightning Source LLC
Chambersburg PA
CBHW021138130626
46554CB00005B/1558